OCT. 07

Investigative Uses of Technology:
Devices, Tools, and Techniques

NCJ 213030

David W. Hagy
Acting Principal Deputy Director, National Institute of Justice

This document was prepared under Interagency Agreement #2003–IJ–R–029 between the National Institute of Justice and the National Institute of Standards and Technology, Office of Law Enforcement Standards.

The National Institute of Justice is a component of the Office of Justice Programs, which also includes the Bureau of Justice Assistance; the Bureau of Justice Statistics; the Community Capacity Development Office; the Office for Victims of Crime; the Office of Juvenile Justice and Delinquency Prevention; and the Office of Sex Offender Sentencing, Monitoring, Apprehending, Registering, and Tracking (SMART).

Technology Working Group for Investigative Uses of High Technology*

Planning panel

James R. Doyle
First Group Associates
New York, New York

Joseph Duke
Drive-Spies, LLC
Clarkston, Michigan

Barry Grundy
Computer Crime Investigator/
 Special Agent
NASA Office of the Inspector General
Office of Investigations
Computer Crimes Division
Goddard Space Flight Center
Greenbelt, Maryland

Keith Hodges
Senior Instructor, Legal Division
Federal Law Enforcement Training Center
Glynco, Georgia

Dan Mares
President
Mares and Company
Lawrenceville, Georgia

Mark J. Menz
M. J. Menz and Associates
Folsom, California

Robert Morgester
Deputy Attorney General
State of California Department of Justice
Office of the Attorney General
Criminal Law Division
Sacramento, California

Phillip Osborn
Senior Special Agent
National Program Manager
Cyber Crimes Center (C3)
Bureau of Immigration and Customs
 Enforcement (ICE)
U.S. Department of Homeland Security
Fairfax, Virginia

John Otero
Lieutenant
Computer Crimes Squad
New York Police Department
New York, New York

David Poole
Chief
Information Operations and Investigations
Air Force Office of Special Investigations
Andrews Air Force Base, Maryland

Michael Weil
Huron Consulting Group
Chicago, Illinois

Technology working group members

Todd Abbott
Vice President
Corporate Information Security
Bank of America
Charlotte, North Carolina

Abigail Abraham
Assistant Attorney General
Illinois Attorney General's Office
Chicago, Illinois

David Arnett
Detective
Arizona Department of Public Safety
Phoenix, Arizona

Dave Ausdenmoore
Detective
Regional Electronics and Computer
  Investigation Section
Hamilton County Sheriff's Office/
  Cincinnati Police Department
Cincinnati, Ohio

Rick Ayers
National Institute of Standards and
  Technology
Gaithersburg, Maryland

Ken Basore
Director of Professional Services
Guidance Software (EnCase)
Reston, Virginia

David Benton
Chief Systems Engineer
Home Depot
Atlanta, Georgia

Walter E. Bruehs
Forensics Examiner
Forensic Audio, Video and Imaging
  Analysis Unit
Federal Bureau of Investigation
Quantico, Virginia

Carleton Bryant
Staff Attorney
Knox County Sheriff's Office
Knoxville, Tennessee

Scott Christensen
Sergeant
Computer Crimes/ICDC Unit
Nebraska State Patrol
Omaha, Nebraska

Bill Crane
Assistant Director
National White Collar Crime Center
Fairmont, West Virginia

Don Flynn
Attorney Advisor
Department of Defense
Cyber Crime Center
Linthicum, Maryland

G.D. Griffin
Assistant Inspector in Charge
Digital Evidence Unit
U.S. Postal Inspection Service
Dulles, Virginia

Amber Haqqani
Director, Digital Evidence
American Academy of Applied Forensics
Central Piedmont Community College
Charlotte, North Carolina

Dave Heslep
Sergeant
Technical Assistance Section Supervisor
Maryland State Police
Technical Investigation Division
Columbia, Maryland

Chip Johnson
Lieutenant
South Carolina Computer Crime Center
Columbia, South Carolina

Nigel Jones
NSLEC Centre for National High Tech
  Crime Training
Wyboston Lakes Business and
  Leisure Centre
Bedfordshire, England

Keith Kelly
Telecommunication Specialist
Washington, D.C.

Tom Kolpacki
Detective
Ann Arbor Police
Livonia, Michigan

Al Lewis
Special Agent
Investigator/DE Examiner
USSS Electronic Crimes Task Force
Chicago, Illinois

Glenn Lewis
Computer Training Specialist
Training Services
SEARCH Group, Inc
Sacramento California

Thomas Musheno
Forensic Examiner
Forensic Audio, Video and Image Analysis
Federal Bureau of Investigation
Engineering Research Facility
Quantico, Virginia

Larissa O'Brien
Chief, Research and Development
Information Operations and Investigations
Air Force Office of Special Investigations
Andrews Air Force Base, Maryland

Timothy O'Shea
Assistant U.S. Attorney
Western District of Wisconsin
Senior Litigation Counsel
Computer Crime and
  Telecommunications Coordinator
Madison, Wisconsin

Thom Quinn
Program Manager
California Department of Justice
Advanced Training Center
Rancho Cordova, California

Henry (Dick) Reeve
General Counsel
Deputy District Attorney
Denver District Attorney's Office
Denver, Colorado

Jim Riccardi, Jr.
Electronic Crime Specialist
CyberScience Lab
National Law Enforcement and
  Corrections Technology Center–Northeast
Rome, New York

Richard Salgado
Senior Counsel
Computer Crime and Intellectual
  Property Section
U.S. Department of Justice
Washington, D.C.

Chris Stippich
President
Digital Intelligence, Inc.
Waukesha, Wisconsin

Facilitators

Susan Ballou
Program Manager for Forensic Sciences
Office of Law Enforcement Standards
National Institute of Standards and
  Technology
Gaithersburg, Maryland

Anjali R. Swienton
President & CEO
SciLawForensics, Ltd.
Germantown, Maryland

*This information reflects each panel member's professional affiliation during the time that the majority of the technology working group's work was performed.

Contents

Introduction

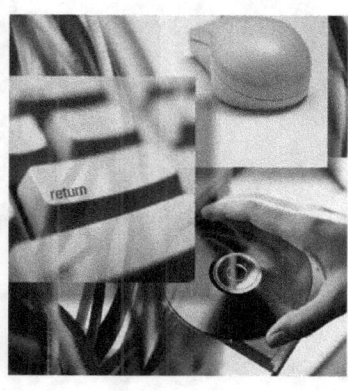

This special report is intended to be a resource to any law enforcement personnel (investigators, first responders, detectives, prosecutors, etc.) who may have limited or no experience with technology-related crimes or with the tools and techniques available to investigate those crimes. It is not all inclusive. Rather, it deals with the most common techniques, devices, and tools encountered.

Technology is advancing at such a rapid rate that the information in this special report must be examined in the context of current technology and practices adjusted as appropriate. It is recognized that all investigations are unique and the judgment of investigators should be given deference in the implementation of this special report. Circumstances of individual cases and Federal, State, and local laws/rules may require actions other than those described in this special report.

When dealing with technology, these general forensic and procedural principles should be applied:

■ Actions taken to secure and collect evidence should not change that evidence.

■ Activity relating to the seizure, examination, storage, or transfer of electronic evidence should be fully documented, preserved, and available for review.

■ Specialized training may be required for the examination of many of the devices described in this special report. Appropriate personnel should be consulted prior to conducting any examination. For more information on the seizure or examination of electronic evidence, see the other special reports in this series: *Electronic Crime Scene Investigation: A Guide for First Responders* (www.ojp.usdoj.gov/nij/pubs-sum/ 187736.htm); *Forensic Examination of Digital Evidence: A Guide for Law Enforcement* (www.ojp.usdoj.gov/nij/pubs-sum/199408.htm); *Digital Evidence in the Courtroom: A Guide for Law Enforcement and Prosecutors* (www.ojp.usdoj.gov/nij/pubs-sum/ 211314.htm); and *Investigations Involving the Internet and Computer Networks* (www.ojp.usdoj.gov/nij/pubs-sum/210798.htm).

Note: All Web links mentioned in this document were active as of the date of publication.

Chapter 1. Techniques

Note: Terms that are defined in the glossary (Appendix A) appear in *bold italics* on their first appearance in the body of the report.

Introduction

This chapter describes a variety of techniques and resources that may help in investigations. The first few pages discuss traditional investigative techniques as they relate to advanced technology, and the following sections provide an awareness of technologies that may affect the investigation.

Law enforcement officers should not be overwhelmed by technology. The presence or availability of technology may enhance the investigation or provide information that may not otherwise be available to the investigator. Although technology can provide significant information, investigators should remember that technology does not replace traditional investigative techniques.

Investigative assistance

Due to the nature of technology, particularly in crimes committed on the Internet, criminal behavior often occurs across jurisdictional boundaries. It is important, therefore, for law enforcement officers to collaborate with other agencies at the Federal, State, and local levels to successfully investigate these types of crimes and apprehend the offenders.

Officers using technology in investigations should also be aware that Federal, State, and local agencies and professional organizations can provide training and technical and investigative assistance. See Appendix B, Technical Resources List, for more information.

Information gathering

Information of investigative value can be collected from a variety of sources including people, places, and things (see chapter 2). The information can be collected through interviews, crime scene and location searches, publicly available information, law enforcement databases, and legal process.

Interviews

While conducting interviews, it is important to determine the victim's, suspect's, or witness's skill level as it relates to technology. The answers to the following questions can affect the investigative plan:

■ What technology (e.g., digital camera, pager, cell phone, computer, **personal digital assistant (PDA)**) did the parties involved have knowledge of, use of, or access to, and at what locations?

■ What is the skill level of the user?

■ What is the security of the device?

— Physical security (e.g., located in a locked facility).

— Data security (e.g., **passphrase protection, firewall**).

■ Who is the owner of the equipment?

■ What accounts, **logins,** and **passwords** are on the device or system?

■ What logs are available (e.g., physical or electronic)?

■ What is the frequency of use (e.g., hardware, software, device, Internet)?

■ How was the device used (e.g., communication device, data storage device)?

■ Is there **offsite storage?** If so, where (physical storage, e.g., backup tapes or disks and/or Internet or **remote data storage**)?

■ Was information transmitted to or shared with other recipients? If so, how (e.g., online, telephone, personal) and to whom?

■ What services or service providers are used?

■ Who is the **system administrator?** Who else may have administrative privileges?

■ Is there remote access to the devices or computer systems?

■ Is the system patched and up to date?

For additional computer- or Internet-related interview questions, consult a technical expert.

Crime scene and location searches

Whether responding to a crime scene or preparing to execute a search warrant, a consideration in the search process is identifying the possible location(s) of information with investigative value. The physical location of the devices or subjects may not necessarily correspond to the location of the data. Information may be found in various locations or may be associated with various devices. In conducting the search, the investigator may want to consider the following:

- Work, personal, or public access devices or systems involved (e.g., work computer, Internet café, library).

- Computer equipment (e.g., computer, PDA, printer, media, **webcam**).

- Computer accessories such as **cradles,** charging devices, batteries, or a notebook computer bag with no computer may indicate the existence of the corresponding supported device.

- Storage media (e.g., **memory cards, ThumbDrives**®).

- Consumer electronics and accessories (e.g., answering machines, cell phones, pagers, fax/scanner/copier machines, digital cameras, caller ID boxes).

- The presence of Internet or network connectivity (e.g., phone, **digital subscriber line (DSL),** and **cable modems; hubs, routers,** and wireless devices).

- Documents or notes containing access information (e.g., user names, passwords) or other evidence.

- Books, manuals, warranty info, and software boxes (indicating potential presence of corresponding devices or software).

- Dumpster diving, trash runs, or recovering abandoned property.

- Bills related to the purchase of products or services.

- Presence of commercial video equipment (e.g., automated teller machines (ATMs)) at or adjacent to the crime scene.

- Alarm or access-control systems.

- Vehicles—presence of **OnStar**®, black box, **global positioning system(GPS), LoJack**®**, EZPass**ˢᴹ**,** or related items.

Note: For information on preservation, collection, and transport of **digital evidence,** see the digital evidence section in this chapter.

Publicly available information

Information may be obtained from the following sources:

- Publicly available government records.

- Internet searches (e.g., **search engines,** Web sites, **newsgroups, discussion groups, chat rooms**).

- ***Internet registries*** (see chapter 2, section on Internet tools to identify users and Internet connections (investigative), overview).

- Commercially available databases of personal and corporate records (e.g., AutoTrak, LexisNexis®, ChoicePoint®, credit bureaus).

Law enforcement databases

In addition to traditional law enforcement resources, several Government-funded databases are available, such as the following:

- Consumer Sentinel (www.FTC.gov).

- Internet Crime Complaint Center (www.IC3.gov).

- Financial Crimes Enforcement Network (http://FINCEN.gov).

- National Center for Missing & Exploited Children (www.NCMEC.org).

Legal process

Legal process may be required to compel the production of certain types of records. State law may impose additional statutory requirements in various forms of compulsory legal process. Types of process are discussed in more detail in Chapter 3, Legal Issues.

Encryption

Encryption may be used to protect or hide important or incriminating data or communications. (See chapter 2, section on encryption tools and passphrase protection.) The best methods for obtaining passwords to decrypt this data are interviews and crime scene searches. With the number of passwords that users are required to remember, a possibility exists that passwords may be stored on paper or other electronic devices.

Digital evidence

Volatility of digital evidence

Digital data are stored in various forms (e.g., ***random access memory (RAM), read only memory (ROM),*** hard drives, and other magnetic or ***optical media***) and are subject to inadvertent alteration, degradation, or loss. Almost any activity performed on a device, whether inadvertent or intentional (e.g., powering up or shutting down), can alter or destroy potential evidence. In addition, loss of battery power in portable devices, changes in magnetic fields, exposure to light, extremes in temperature, and even rough handling can cause loss of data. Due to these factors, steps should be taken in a timely manner to preserve data.

Special precautions should be taken when documenting, collecting, preserving, and examining digital evidence. Failure to do so may render it unusable, result in an inaccurate conclusion, or affect its admissibility or persuasiveness. Consult a trained professional if any questions arise about handling specific digital devices or media. Activities that should be avoided include the following:

- Putting a Post-it® note (adhesive material) on the surface of a CD or **floppy disk**.

- Using permanent markers to label CDs.

- Placing magnetic media close to strong magnetic fields (e.g ., radio equipment in car trunks, electric motors, computer monitors).

- Placing magnetic media in high-temperature environments.

- Exposing optical media (e.g., **CD-ROMs**) to light or high-temperature environments.

- Exposing media to static electricity (e.g., transporting or storing media in plastic bags, photocopying).

- Rough handling of a seemingly sturdy container (e.g., hard drives, laptop computers).

STOP Wireless devices in use by law enforcement should be disabled prior to entering a search site to avoid communicating (pairing) with subject devices.

STOP Subjects may boobytrap electronic devices to cause data loss or personal injury. Explosive devices have been placed inside computer cases and set to detonate when the on/off switch is pressed.

STOP Many electronic devices contain memory that requires continuous power (such as a battery or AC power) to maintain information. Data can be easily lost by unplugging the power source or allowing the battery to discharge. To avoid this, place the device in its charger or immediately replace the batteries. If custody of the device is transferred, receiving personnel must be alerted to the power requirements of the device.

Importance of digital evidence

Data and records obtained from digital media and Internet usage can yield significant investigative leads. Digital information should be handled in a manner that includes a fully documented chain of custody initiated at the point of seizure. Analysis of digital evidence should be performed on a forensic duplicate by trained personnel while maintaining the integrity of the original evidence. Federal, State, and local agencies; government resources; private entities; or academic institutions may have capabilities that can assist with the analysis of the following:

- Computer forensic examinations. A discussion of computer forensic capabilities can be found in *Forensic Examination of Digital Evidence: A Guide for Law Enforcement* (www.ojp.usdoj.gov/nij/pubs-sum/199408.htm). An examination of electronic media can reveal the following:

— Registered ownership and software registration information.

— Journals, diaries, and logs.

— Databases, spreadsheets, pictures, and documents.

— Deleted and **hidden files.**

— Internet activity.

— Communications-user input (e.g., e-mail, **chat logs**).

— Communications-data transfers (e.g., **peer to peer (P2P),** newsgroups)

— Financial records.

— Data to be used in a timeline analysis.

— Contraband.

- Audio analysis. Audio recordings obtained by law enforcement may contain ambient noise that interferes with interpretation. Technology exists to analyze and improve the quality of the recordings.

- Video analysis. Video recordings obtained by law enforcement are often surveillance tapes, which are multiplexed (multiple or split-screen views), proprietary in format, will need to be viewed on a specific **platform,** or are of poor quality. Technology exists to analyze and improve the quality of the recorded images. The technology may be available from the manufacturer or end user of the video equipment.

- Picture analysis. Technology exists to analyze and improve the quality of still images. The technology may be available from the manufacturer or end user of the equipment.

Electronic communications

Electronic communications (e.g., e-mail, text messaging, picture messaging) may be available from **Internet service providers (ISPs),** pager companies, cellular or wireless phone service providers, public access (e.g., **wireless hotspots,** Internet cafes, public libraries, academic institutions), and suspect or victim computers.

E-mail

E-mail can be the starting point or a key element in many investigations. It is the electronic equivalent of a letter or a memo and may include attachments or enclosures. E-mail can provide many investigative leads, including the following:

- Possible point of origin, which can lead to the suspect's location.

- Identification of the account, which can lead to the suspect.

— Investigators can proactively communicate with a suspect to gather identifying information (e.g., an e-mail can be sent to communicate with a suspect and ultimately to establish identity).

■ Transactional information related to the Internet connection.

■ Direct evidence of the crime (e.g., the content of communications between suspect and victim may be contained in an e-mail).

For investigative purposes, the complete *e-mail header* information may be needed for optimum results. For additional information see *Investigations Involving the Internet and Computer Networks* (www.ojp.usdoj.gov/nij/pubs-sum/210798.htm).

STOP Refer to Chapter 3, Legal Issues, for the legal process required to obtain this information.

Online chat and messaging

Electronic communication services allow people to communicate in real time using a variety of applications (e.g., *Internet relay chat (IRC), instant messaging (IM), AOL Instant Messenger™,* Windows Messenger, *ICQ).* These communications may involve text, voice, video, and file transfers and may reveal the following:

■ Possible point of origin, which could lead to the suspect's location.

■ Identification of the suspect through a screen name.

■ Transactional information related to the Internet connection.

■ Direct evidence of the crime (e.g., the content of communications between suspect and victim may be contained in an *online chat*).

■ Identifying information about the suspect (by using online *chat programs* to proactively communicate with a suspect).

STOP Refer to Chapter 3, Legal Issues, for the legal process required to obtain this information.

Proactive undercover operations

■ The Internet may be used to facilitate undercover operations such as the investigation of child exploitation and the trafficking of contraband.

■ Specialized training and legal counsel may be required to engage in these operations. Various Federal and State organizations can provide guidance or assistance.

> **Note:** Law enforcement must take special precautions when using the Internet in an undercover role. E-mails and chat activity contain encoded information that can reveal the identity of the sender or the computer the sender used. Visiting a Web site may leave behind this same coded information revealing who (or what computer) visited the Web site. Computers and identities used in undercover operations should not be attributable to an agency network or individual.

Web site records (e.g., FedEx®, PayPal®)

Web sites often track the **Internet Protocol (IP) address,** time, date of access of the user, and other information. For example, **PayPal®** and FedEx® have transaction records related to the sale and purchase of a product or service. Investigators should request these records be preserved or obtain these records in a timely manner because they may only be maintained for a short period of time.

 Refer to Chapter 3, Legal Issues, for further information.

Service provider records

Account records may be maintained for a limited amount of time or not at all. Therefore, a law enforcement investigator may compel that the records be preserved pursuant to 18 U.S.C. § 2703(f). With proper legal process and sufficient information (e.g., username or IP address and date/time), the service provider may be able to provide the following information:

- Subscriber information (e.g., name and address).

- Method of payment and billing information.

- Transactional data (connection log, e.g., location, time, caller ID of dial-in location, and duration of connection to the Internet).

- Content of communications.

- Miscellaneous (e.g., additional screen names on account, **buddy lists,** e-mail forwarding).

 Refer to Chapter 3, Legal Issues, for the legal process required to obtain this information.

Voice over Internet Protocol

Voice over Internet Protocol (Voice over IP/VoIP) allows computer users to make telephone calls over the Internet or computer **networks.** Communications providers that offer VoIP may maintain subscriber information and transactional information concerning these connections. This information may be obtained using the same legal process used to obtain information from an ISP, but the nonconsensual real-time interception of the content of these communications may require a wiretap order.

STOP Refer to Chapter 3, Legal Issues, for the legal process required to obtain this information.

Telecommunications

Public telephone networks provide telecommunication services through a variety of computer and consumer electronic devices like PDAs, cell phones, and others. Investigators and telecommunications companies are guided by the authority and constraints of *Title III* and the *Communications Assistance for Law Enforcement Act of 1994 (CALEA)*.

STOP Specific orders for the production of the following types of information are addressed in Chapter 3, Legal Issues.

Cell tower data (cell site data)

Cellular telephone tower data are available to law enforcement and may provide valuable information regarding the specific location of the phone of a particular subscriber being investigated. These records are stored with the provider of phone service and generally exist through one billing cycle.

Portable communications devices

These devices (e.g., wireless phones, PDAs, pagers) can store address books, phone lists, e-mail addresses, message content, pictures, audio files, most recent incoming and outgoing calls, and appointment books and journals, and can perform almost any other function found on a home computer.

Data contained on these devices may be volatile because of battery life. Adequate protective steps must be taken to ensure preservation of potential evidence. See chapter 2, section on power concerns with battery-operated devices, for additional information, or immediately contact personnel trained in the seizure and analysis of this type of digital evidence for assistance.

Answering machines, answering services, and voice mail

Answering machines, answering services, and voice mail can provide valuable information (see chapter 2, section on answering machines and voice mail systems, for more information). The legal procedure for obtaining the data from these sources differs depending on the location of the information and the people who have access to it.

Refer to Chapter 3, Legal Issues, for the legal process required to obtain this information.

Video surveillance

With the proliferation of video surveillance systems, it is increasingly likely that public conduct will be captured on video. Video security systems have been put in place by businesses, government entities, and private citizens. To discover these systems, law enforcement officers should carefully look for cameras and inquire of the businesses if they have surveillance equipment.

Security and traffic cameras

Cameras can be found in airports, convenience stores, public roadways and intersections, businesses, bus and rail depots, banks, ATMs, etc. These camera systems may capture activity inside and outside the area where they are located. As with other electronic evidence, the tapes or recordings should be obtained as soon as possible to ensure that the data are not overwritten or destroyed. The information that can be obtained from these cameras includes the following:

- Presence of subjects.

- Vehicle or license plate information.

- Support of witness or suspect statements.

- Timeline of events.

- Commission of the crime.

- Subject activities.

Note: Video surveillance recordings are often of poor quality, multiplexed (multiple or split-screen views), or may be recorded in a proprietary format requiring a special platform for viewing. Investigators should take the appropriate steps to be able to view the data at a later time.

Law enforcement use of cameras

Cameras can be placed in public areas to deter criminal activity and to capture or monitor illegal activity. With legal authority, cameras can be placed in locations where there is a reasonable expectation of privacy.

Criminals' use of cameras

Criminals use cameras for three purposes:

- Conducting illegal activities, such as recording child pornography or videotaping people where they have a reasonable expectation of privacy.

- Conducting surveillance and countersurveillance. Criminals may employ surveillance techniques against law enforcement, including audio and video surveillance and alarm systems. Law enforcement should be aware of this potential threat when conducting investigations.

- Recording criminal acts. Criminals often pose with weapons and drugs and record their criminal activity, such as rapes or murders.

Consensual monitoring

Consensual monitoring is the monitoring of **wire,** oral, or electronic communication with the knowledge and consent of at least one involved party. Some States, however, are more restrictive in that they require the consent of all parties to the communication. Intercepts that may be considered consensual monitoring in some States may require legal process elsewhere. Consult with a prosecutor in the relevant jurisdiction for guidance. Examples of wire, oral, and electronic communications that may involve consensual monitoring include the following:

- Telephone conversations—wire.

- Personal communications—oral (e.g., **parabolic microphones, body wires**).

- Computer communications—electronic (e.g., **keystroke monitoring, sniffer** output).

    — To monitor computer communications, consent may be implied through the use of written user agreements or through legally sufficient **banners** that inform the users that their activities are being monitored.

Tracking

Tracking systems provide law enforcement the ability to track the movement or identify the location of persons or objects. A search warrant or a court order may be required. Consult with your local prosecutor for specific guidance on this issue. Examples of tracking systems include the following:

- **GPS.** (See chapter 2, section on GPS devices, for more information.) GPS satellites can establish the location of the item being tracked. Once the location is established, this information may be transferred to the law enforcement officer via radio frequency or cellular frequencies, or the position may simply be logged within the device. Real-time tracking is possble with some devices. Generally, the positions are integrated with a software system that displays the track on a map.

- **Directional find (DF)/radio frequency (RF).** Radio transmitters can be placed on or in packages, persons, or vehicles, which can then be tracked in real time using direction-finding receivers (e.g., LoJack®, BirdDog®).

- **Commercially available vehicle tracking systems.** Some consumer products have tracking devices built into them by the manufacturer. These devices are especially prevalent in vehicles (e.g., vehicle black box, OnStar®). These devices may record speed, location, or brake usage. They may also provide direct communication with persons in the vehicle.

- **Some States provide electronic devices that allow passage through tolls.** These systems capture the date and time of toll passage (e.g., EZPass℠, Telco).

- **Access-control systems.** (See chapter 2, section on access-control devices, for more information). Access-control systems allow entry into secure areas and track employee movements. These systems can record date and time of entry and user information. These systems include key cards, retinal scanners, fingerprint scanners, voice recognition systems, and similar items.

- **Credit or membership cards.** Use of these cards creates a record, which may provide information related to the geographic location and travel history for the use of the card (e.g., hotel, gas, airline), as well as date/time/location of the item purchased.

Throughout this publication, scenarios may be provided to illustrate the uses of specific devices or techniques.

Practical example

Note: This scenario is presented as an example, not as the only way to conduct an investigation.

On March 15, your agency or department is contacted by a local power station whose management advises that it has discovered child pornography images on one of the computers in its control room. You respond to the station and discover that it is located in a large office building and that the computer in question is located in an unsecured open office area accessible to all employees (approximately 300), but assigned to the exclusive use of 8 accounting employees. Company management copied the 60 suspected child pornography images to floppy disks and turns them over to you. Unfortunately, management reformatted the computer's hard drive prior to your arrival in an effort to permanently remove the offending material and placed the computer back in service.

The investigation:

1. Evidence preservation

The floppy disks containing the child pornography images are secured and write protected, and the chain of custody is documented. Evidence that may identify the individual responsible for the images, as well as additional evidence of criminal activity, could be located in different areas of the hard drive. You know that reformatting the computer's hard drive will not necessarily destroy potential evidence, but continued use of the computer might. In this case, management signs a consent form to search the computer. Without consent, exigent circumstances, such as potential loss of evidence through the continued use of the computer, would have allowed you to seize the computer and apply for a search warrant.

Key points to consider:

- Volatility of data if not seized.

- Consent versus search warrant.

- Chain of custody.

2. Interviewing

You conduct interviews with station management to collect information as to the who, what, when, where, how, and why of the incident. Management advises you that one of the employees (Dave Jones) discovered the child pornography in a download directory on the computer while conducting some Internet research using Acme Online. Jones immediately reported his discovery to management. Management advises you that the station maintains an Acme Online account for research purposes and that only two employees had access to the account. One of the employees is Jones, the other is a lineman named Mike Smith. Management tells you that they believe that Smith is responsible for the child pornography because of several incidents within the past year involving Smith and his obvious preoccupation with children. This preoccupation involved Smith's operation of a child talent agency as a side business and a previous arrest for public sexual misconduct involving a minor that management only recently discovered. Smith was fired just days before the discovery of the child pornography. Management advises that the screen names associated with the Acme Online account are DaveyJ123 (Jones), and MikeyS123 (Smith).

Investigative steps:

- Ask station management to preserve the access logs to the building and the station's computer network.

- Issue preservation letter to Acme Online.

  — Determine retention policies of the ISP.

- Determine whether network storage or backup data exist for involved systems (e.g., tapes, etc.) and, if so, request their preservation or consider seizing them.

- Obtain consent or other legal process for Acme Online and the station's records.

- Obtain the station's computer use policy document.

  — Do they have one?

  — Is there documentation that the subject had knowledge of the policy?

- Determine whether there are other devices to which the suspect may have had access.

- Determine whether management disabled his access to the Acme account.

3. Computer forensics

A forensic examination of the floppy disks and of the computer's hard drive reveals child pornography images. Analysis of the child pornography files indicates that they were downloaded to the computer on three consecutive days: January 1, 2, and 3, and between 3 a.m. and 5:30 a.m. on all 3 days.

Key point to consider:

- Processing of the evidence should be done by a trained forensic examiner.

4. Records collection

The station building security office advises that employees have individually assigned passkey cards for building access. You request the building access records for the period of December 31 through January 4.

You also request telephone billing records from station management for the telephone line attached to the suspect computer for the same time period.

You obtain appropriate legal process for the production of Acme Online account records associated with the Acme Online account.

You request and obtain work schedule records for the station employees.

Key points to consider:

- Inquire regarding video surveillance at the station to establish suspect's use of assigned key card.

- Inquire whether any duplicate access cards have been issued.

5. Records analysis

The station building access records indicate that Smith's access card was the only access card used to enter and exit the building during the 3 a.m. to 5:30 a.m. timeframe on each of the nights the files were downloaded. Analysis of employee timesheets and schedules indicate that Smith was scheduled and worked a 9 a.m. to 5 p.m. day shift during the same period.

Telephone billing records for the phone line attached to the computer indicate connections to a local Acme Online access number during the 3 a.m. to 5:30 a.m. time period in question.

Acme Online records indicate that the MikeyS123 account was active on each of the three nights in question and at the times associated with the child pornography file downloads.

6. Investigation and search warrants

Smith's Department of Motor Vehicles records and employee records identify his residence address.

Trash runs (dumpster diving) conducted on Smith's residence reveal fragments of broken floppy disks, empty floppy disk boxes, and several computer software manuals.

Analysis of records obtained from Acme Online pursuant to a search warrant discloses child pornography e-mail attachments associated with the MikeyS123 screen name. No child pornography is associated with the reporting source's screen name of DaveyJ123. Further analysis finds that some of the e-mail from the MikeyS123 account details an ongoing communication with another Acme Online subscriber named TonyGTTT123. In these communications MikeyS123 was found to be trading child pornography graphics with this other subscriber and identified himself as Mike Smith of Virginia. MikeyS123 even provided a cellular telephone number in one communication for further contact. Telephone subscriber records verify that this number had belonged to Smith, the station employee.

Based on your investigation, you request and obtain a search warrant for Smith's apartment to search for computer and child pornography evidence. On execution of the warrant, however, you discover that Smith has fled the area.

Key points to consider:

- Note that the MikeyS123 account was established through the employer's Acme Online account.

- Expand the child pornography investigation to include TonyGTTT123 and to identify any other accounts that Smith is using to communicate with TonyGTTT123.

- Aspects of the investigation may lead to outside jurisdiction. Investigators may have to contact appropriate law enforcement agencies for assistance.

- Obtain appropriate cellular records that may lead to Smith's location.

7. E-mail pen/trap and trace

Apply for an e-mail trap and trace on the Acme Online account for the subscriber TonyGTTT123. Analysis of the e-mail addresses of the subscriber's sent and received e-mail reveals ongoing communications with several individuals.

A search of the Acme Online membership directory identifies the profiles of the Acme Online subscribers communicating with TonyGTTT123. One member is identified as using the screen name of LittleMS123 whose profile lists the user's name as Mike Smith, photographer and owner of a child talent agency in the Anytown, USA, area.

Records obtained pursuant to additional legal process issued to Acme Online for the account associated with LittleMS123 reflect that an account has been established in the name of Mike Smith. The account was established using a credit card associated with the mother of the suspect. Access records from Acme Online indicate that this account regularly uses a local Acme Online dial-up access number in the Anytown, USA, area.

Key points to consider:

▪ Records relating to the dial-up access number may reveal a possible location for Smith.

▪ Be aware that counterfeit, stolen, or fraudulent identification may be used to create user accounts.

▪ Be aware that multiple users may use the same account with different screen names and may use the account from different locations.

8. Undercover activity

To locate the suspect, you use an undercover Acme Online account through a local **Internet Crimes Against Children (ICAC) Task Force.** You make regular undercover access to Acme Online over several days. Searches for the LittleMS123 screen name eventually locate the suspect in a chat room in the Anytown, USA, area. Engaging the suspect in an online conversation, you convince the suspect that you will be traveling to the Anytown, USA, area soon, and you request and receive his telephone number to arrange a meeting on your arrival. During these online chats with the suspect, which are all properly logged and memorialized, the suspect indicates a preference for children and transmits several pornographic images to you of children engaged in sexual activities.

Key points to consider:

▪ Be sure to use a covert account for undercover activities (i.e., communications should not be traceable to a home or agency computer).

▪ Specialized training may be required to document undercover or online activities properly.

▪ Agency and legal authorization may be needed for conducting undercover activity.

9. The apprehension

Records obtained through legal process served on the telephone company for the dial-up access identify an address in the Anytown, USA, area. Physical surveillance of the address identifies Smith's car parked in the driveway. An application for a search warrant is made for the address and is ordered by the court. Sought in the search warrant are the child pornography files received from the suspect during your online communications, the child pornography from the station computer, and all records containing communication with, for, or about children. The warrant also includes the authority to search for,

seize, and examine any computer or other data storage devices and media that could contain child pornography evidence or other records.

During the execution of the search warrant, Smith is located in the residence. In addition, several computers with attached modems, two digital still cameras, a digital camcorder, several audio cassettes, an analog answering machine, a cellular phone, several analog video cassettes, and several hundred laserjet prints of child pornography images are seized. Several of the printed images appear to be identical to the images from the station computer.

You arrest Smith and read him the Miranda warnings. He waives his rights and agrees to answer questions. Smith provides you his password and states that he is the sole user of this account. You send a preservation request to Acme Online for Smith's account and apply for a warrant a few days later.

Key points to consider:

- Review Chapter 3, Legal Issues, for additional information.

10. Postarrest investigation

During booking, Smith is found to be wearing a watch that is capable of storing data, including photographs. Analysis of this watch and Smith's digital camera reveal images of children engaged in sexual acts. Enhancement of the images is done to produce identifiable images of the victims' faces.

Analysis of the answering machines and audio cassette tapes reveals the recorded voices of several adults arranging a photo session for their children with Smith involving his talent agency business. Telephone numbers recovered from Smith's cell phone are traced. This contact information eventually leads to the identification of some of the children depicted in the photos recovered from Smith's camera.

Forensic analysis of the computers seized identify numerous child pornography files, as well as evidence that these files were printed on Smith's laser printer.

Key points to consider:

- **Preservation order** to cell phone provider for stored voice mail and subscriber information.

- A warrant may be necessary to access the data stored in the watch.

- Similar to the watch, a variety of small wearable devices are capable of storing data. See Chapter 2, Tools and Devices, for more information.

Chapter 2. Tools and Devices

Introduction

This chapter is designed to provide a general description of the technology-related tools and devices that either may be encountered in an investigation or may assist in the identification and examination of electronic evidence. For ease of use, tools and devices are arranged alphabetically. An overview of their function and usefulness is provided, and other special investigative considerations are discussed. Where applicable, this chapter describes how persons use these devices to facilitate the commission of crimes. The reader is encouraged to think creatively about a device and consider all possible investigative uses and forms a device may take.

Because devices can be multifunctional, investigators should ensure that all relevant devices and storage media are collected. For example, as explained in this chapter, some watches have data storage capability (see section on removable storage media and players), and some cell phones can perform camera functions (see section on cell phones). As more functions converge into a single device, investigators should be aware that relevant information can be stored in seemingly mundane or commonplace objects or devices.

Devices can also be modified to perform functions beyond those intended by the manufacturer. For example, the Microsoft Xbox® is designed to play video games but can be altered to store data and can be modified to be a fully functional computer. In other cases, devices are physically altered to perform functions completely different from their original purpose. For example, cellular phones, pagers, and pens have been altered to be firearms; narcotics have been stored in hollowed-out personal digital assistant (PDA) styli. The investigator should be aware of the surroundings of the device to gain clues as to the likelihood that it has been altered. (See Appendix C, Hacked Devices.)

Power concerns with battery-operated devices

STOP Many electronic devices contain memory that requires continuous power (such as a battery or AC power) to maintain information. Data can be easily lost by unplugging the power source or allowing the battery to discharge. To avoid this, place the device in its charger or immediately replace the batteries. If custody of the device is transferred, receiving personnel must be alerted to the power requirements of the device.

Some small electronic devices, such as PDAs, connect or synchronize data to more powerful devices such as computers. Some of the small devices have two cords or sit in cradles with two cords, one for power and one for data transfer. For some devices, one cord both permits data transfer and provides power. It is not always possible to tell by looking at the cord whether it allows data transfer functions, supplies power, or does both. Be sure to determine the use and need of all cables attached to the device. Check the manufacturer's Web site for standard configurations.

If the investigator seizing a device is unsure whether the connection performs both functions, it is safer to provide power to the device by replacing the batteries, if possible. If replacing the batteries on a timely basis is impractical, be aware of the risk that data transfer may occur if the device is connected to another electronic device and both devices are running. If the investigator chooses to connect two devices (or leave two devices connected), it is critical that this is documented and that both devices and connectors are seized if legally permitted. The person performing data recovery should be notified of the investigator's actions.

The investigator also should be aware that some devices have passwords that are activated when the PDA is powered off or goes into **sleep mode.** Those passwords can be difficult to defeat.

Access-control devices

A traditional-access control device that uses preprogrammed personal information on a card in combination with a personal identification number (PIN) to allow access to restricted areas.

A biometric device (fingerprint reader) that allows access to the device to which the mouse is attached.

Introduction

Access-control devices attempt to authenticate the identity of an individual. Authentication is based on one or more elements of the following triad: "Something you have, something you know, something you are." Key fobs and **smart cards** are "something you have": a physical object that establishes identity. These devices may work by being inserted into a reader or by "proximity readers," which detect the key fob or smart card at a distance. Keypads require "something you know," generally a passcode. Biometric devices evaluate "something you are" by measuring or assessing a person-specific physical characteristic. **Biometric devices** include iris or retina scanners, fingerprint scanners, face or voice recognition, gait detectors, and hand geometry detectors.

Value of access-control devices

- Investigators can use these to do the following:

  — Help establish the presence or absence of an individual at a controlled location (as in identity theft and espionage cases).

  — Monitor patterns or profiles of activity that may be malicious.

- Subjects can additionally use these to do the following:

  — Gain unauthorized access to a physical location.

  — Create false alibis by implying that people were somewhere that they were not.

Identifying and obtaining access-control devices

- Access-control devices can take the form of key fobs, keypads, smart cards, or biometric sensing devices (e.g., those that measure fingerprints, gait, voice, and unique physical characteristics).

- Keypads and biometric devices are usually mounted on a wall or counter outside a restricted area. They may also be mounted near the exit to a restricted area if the outlet is controlled.

- These devices can all be purchased from a variety of sources.

- Although data may be stored on the device, usually data are stored on a centralized database.

Special investigatory and other considerations

- Data may be overwritten in a centralized database. Data may be remotely purged if suspect(s) remain at large.

- Key fobs or smart cards may be demagnetized.

- Biometrics may be affected by physical injury or alterations (e.g., retinal patterns may change during pregnancy).

- Note that key fobs, smart cards, and passcodes can be stolen or compromised, so a device's records or logs may be unreliable.

- Biometrics have defined failure rates and may not definitively establish the presence or absence of an individual.

Legal considerations

■ General Fourth Amendment principles apply.

■ Having the technical ability to use an access-control device does not always mean that the device may be accessed without legal process.

Scenarios

1. A suspect has given an alibi claiming to have been at work when the crime was committed. The company where the suspect works uses key card access devices. By examining the key card log files, it is determined that the suspect was not at work as claimed.

2. A homicide suspect offered an alibi to the police claiming to be at home during the time of the murder. The police officers determined that the suspect had a home alarm system. They obtained the information pertaining to the time the alarm was set and the time it was disarmed. Those times corroborated the suspect's alibi.

3. An adult is missing and presumed kidnapped. Examination of the bank automated teller machine (ATM) records reveals use of the victim's ATM card. Surveillance video of the ATM shows the victim was alone while withdrawing the cash. Credit card transactions also reveal motel stays along the same route in which the ATM transactions were conducted.

Answering machines and voice mail systems (digital and analog)

No tape (digital)

With tape (analog)

Introduction

An answering machine records voice messages from callers when the called party is unavailable or declines to answer a telephone call, usually plays a message from the called party before recording a message, and often retains date and time stamp information. An answering machine may have multiple settings, users, or voice boxes; may be built into a telephone; or may be a separate device. Voice mail messages may also be stored on an onsite device or located remotely at a communication service provider.

Value of answering machines and voice mail systems

- Investigators can use these to do the following:

  - Obtain actual recordings of telephone call content and date/time stamp of the message, and determine whether the message has been listened to or not.

  - Identify callers by content of incoming messages.

  - Identify owners by prerecorded outgoing messages.

  - Establish undercover identities.

  - Covertly monitor incoming calls in threat or stalking investigations.

- Subjects can additionally use these to do the following:

  - Alter or erase original recordings to redirect or mislead investigators.

  - Facilitate and lend credibility to criminal enterprise.

  - Communicate with one another.

Identifying and obtaining answering machines and voice mail systems

- Home-based answering machines can be found at retail outlets.

- Voice mail systems for businesses may be purchased from major computer and telecommunications equipment suppliers.

- Voice mail service can be acquired through telephone companies or communications service providers.

- Voice over Internet Protocol (VoIP) is a form of Internet-based telephony and can be acquired through an Internet service provider (ISP) or another Internet-based service. VoIP may include services similar to those found in voice mail systems.

Special investigatory and other considerations

- Information can be remotely purged or altered, anyone with the password can access the systems, and there may be automatic destruction policies.

- Backed-up data may be accessible for long timeframes if an investigator is seeking voice mail at a business.

- Remove the telephone cord from a local answering machine to prevent remote purging.

- Data on answering machines may be subject to loss if the device loses power. Consider using a tape recorder to record messages before removing power.

- Day, date, and time settings found on the device should be verified against the actual day, date, and time.

Legal considerations

- General principles regarding the Fourth Amendment apply to stored communications on the device.

- Prior to obtaining remotely stored electronic communications (e.g., voice mail stored by a third-party provider), see Chapter 3, Legal Issues, for **Electronic Communications Privacy Act (ECPA)** issues.

- With devices having multiple mailboxes, privacy issues related to consent may exist. For more information on stored communications, see Chapter 3, Legal Issues.

Scenario

During a homicide investigation, the suspect offered a voice mail message with date and time stamp as an alibi. Subsequent investigation of the company's voice mail system revealed that the time settings did not coincide with the actual time because the system had not been adjusted to account for daylight savings time; therefore, the suspect's alibi was invalidated.

Audio: Digital tools used to conduct examinations of audio formats

Introduction

Investigations may involve the seizure or preservation (e.g., recordings during an undercover investigation) of audio recordings that need to be analyzed or enhanced. This section discusses the tools that will assist in maximizing the evidentiary value of digital or analog recordings. These tools and devices aid in the acquisition, processing, and output of audio information.

Value of digital tools used to conduct examinations of audio formats

- Investigators may use these tools to do the following:

  — Enhance a recording to:

    - Make it more intelligible.

    - Eliminate, isolate, or enhance background noise (e.g., to identify location of the call).

  — Authenticate a recording to determine:

    - The source or origin.

    - Whether a recording has been altered.

— Determine the time, sequence, and direction of the source of sounds on a recording .

— Convert a recording to other formats (e.g., convert analog to digital).

■ Subjects may additionally use these tools to do the following:

— Alter original recordings, as most of the tools considered here are ine xpensive and publicly available.

Identifying and obtaining the digital tools used to conduct examinations of audio formats

■ The tools needed to examine digital audio formats depend on the types of examinations that are being conducted.

■ Software, hardware, and professional-grade signal-processing equipment that are commonly used in the examinations can be acquired from vendors, retail stores, or professional recording supply houses.

Special investigatory and other considerations

■ Various degrees of training are needed to use these tools to conduct audio e xaminations. A wide range of computer skill levels are needed to operate most of the hardware and software used in these examinations. Advanced skills are needed to analyze and interpret audio data.

■ Examiners should have the original recordings available, but where feasible, examinations should be made on a copy. If work on the original is necessary, consider seeking legal guidance prior to the examination.

■ Consult someone with specific expertise in this area.

Legal considerations

■ Software tools should have appropriate licensing agreements.

■ There are generally no other legal considerations provided that the recording being examined has been lawfully acquired.

Scenario

A telephonic bomb threat to a school was recorded. An audio examination and enhancement of the recording identified noises in the background that indicated the call came from a video arcade. Another voice was identified in the background; when analyzed, the person could be heard placing a phone order in whic h the arcade's address was mentioned. This led investigators to the site and facilitated the apprehension of the suspect.

Caller ID devices

Caller ID devices display the telephone
number(s) of incoming calls.

Introduction

Caller ID-enabled devices record telephone numbers and other information associated
with inbound telephone calls. Information recorded by these devices may include the
date/time stamp and the name of the registered user. Caller ID service must first be
activated by the telephone company for the information to be received. Some caller ID
devices may be programmed to block certain telephone numbers. The data stored are
generally local to the device, but some data may be stored at the service provider.
Date/time information that comes from a service provider is more likely to be accurate
than information stored on the device itself. Memory is often limited and content may be
lost with the removal of power.

STOP The telephone number that the device records may not be the one from which the
call originated due to the use of prepaid telephone cards, trunk lines, inaccurate information from the telephone company, etc.

Value of caller ID devices

- Investigators can use these to do the following:

  — Determine the date, time, and source of incoming calls (e.g ., to establish or
    contradict an alibi or identify coconspirators).

- Subjects can additionally use these to do the following:

  — Determine who is calling them, including calls from law enforcement officers,
    undercover agents, and confidential informants.

  — Manipulate the date, time, and other information on the caller ID device to support
    false alibis.

Identifying and obtaining caller ID devices

- External caller ID devices must be attached to a telephone line.

- The caller ID function can be integrated into telephones, computers, cellular phones, satellite television receivers, and other telecommunication devices (e.g., PDAs).

- Caller ID devices are commercially available.

Special investigatory and other considerations

- Consider contacting the phone company to learn about the subject's phone service features, including information about caller ID or use of call blocker.

- Investigators should be aware that subjects may identify them through caller ID and that call blocking on their phone may be defeated by the subject's use of the automatic redial feature. Check with the relevant telephone service provider for further information. Always use an undercover phone when calling suspects.

- Caller ID devices have limited capacity and only retain a certain number of incoming numbers. The most recent calls may overwrite older calls previously stored in the device.

- Some caller ID devices may not register each inbound call as a separate number when the same telephone number calls repeatedly. In such cases, some notation by the number may show multiple calls.

- Some dial-up ISPs include call waiting when users are connected to the Internet, which displays the number of the incoming call. In such cases, some caller ID information may be stored on the computer.

- Some caller ID devices require a constant power supply. Data may be lost if the power is interrupted. When seizing the device, determine whether the device has a battery. If so, install a fresh battery prior to unplugging it.

- When legal authority exists, all data stored on the device should be reviewed, photographed, and recorded before disconnecting the power.

- When calling a toll-free number (e.g., 800), caller ID blocking (*67) may not be enabled since the recipient is paying for the call.

Legal considerations

- Seizing or searching caller ID devices implicates Fourth Amendment concerns.

- In lieu of using the caller ID device, law enforcement may obtain records from the communications provider, including local and long-distance call records.

- A trap and trace or pen register order is needed for future nonconsensual capture of incoming and outgoing phone numbers. (For more information, see Chapter 3, Legal Issues.)

Cell phones

Integrated cell phone, PDA with e-mail, text messaging, Web browsing, and digital camera

Traditional cell phone with scheduling features

Video phone

Media phones incorporate video streaming and playback, along with audio capture, cell phone, camera, PDA, and Internet communication (e.g , e-mail, Web browsing, etc.).

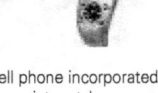

A standard cell phone incorporated into a wrist watch

Bluetooth®-enabled wireless headset

Introduction

Cell phones are handheld portable, battery-operated devices that are becoming increasingly sophisticated and incorporate features found in many other electronic devices. They generally have keypads, small LCD screens, and some sort of antennae. The data stored are usually local to the device, although some data may be stored at the service provider. Some telephones have a push-to-talk or walkie-talkie feature.

Value of cell phones

■ Investigators can use these to do the following:

— Obtain the following information when they have access to a subject's cell phone or information retained by the cell phone service provider:

- Calls made, received, and missed.

- Telephone number of the device.

- ***Electronic serial number (ESN).***

- Text messages.

- E-mail messages.

- Voice mail.

- Call logs (date/time of calls, duration).

- Saved dialing directories (e.g., stored phone book, speed-dial information).

- Digital images and video.

- GPS information to include searches or directions saved.

- Suspect movement through cell tracking information.

- Purchase information.

- Subscriber information.

— Obtain stored data that may be unrelated to telecommunications such as calendars, tasks, and notes. This information may be stored internally on the device or on removable media (see section on removable storage media and players). Storage capability on cell phones is constantly increasing.

— Use cell phones as a substitute for a body wire.

— Function as Web browsers. The information normally obtained from a computer's browser may be available from a Web-enabled phone.

— Send and receive e-mail and text messages. The information available from the telephone itself will be similar to that found on a computer used for e-mail.

— Track, in real time, the cell phone's location through cell towers or through the use of GPS-enabled phones.

STOP Consider submitting the telephone to trained personnel for forensic examination to extract all data from the device.

■ Subjects may additionally use these to do the following:

— Avoid detection through the use of prepaid services and disposable or stolen phones.

— Covertly listen to conversations.

— Trigger explosive devices.

— Conceal explosive devices and firearms.

Identifying and obtaining cell phones

■ Cell phones have been incorporated into headset-only devices, wrist watches, and PDAs. They are most commonly kept on or near a person or an immediately accessible container such as a purse or briefcase or charging device.

■ Cell phones are commercially available.

■ Cell phones are frequently stolen, used for a short period of time, and then discarded.

■ Some phones have removable digital media. Removable media should be identified, obtained, and examined as appropriate.

Special investigatory and other considerations

■ Data may be retained on the telephone itself, in removable media, or at the service provider.

■ Information held by the service provider is time sensitive. There are no standardized or required retention periods for this information. Failure to preserve or obtain the information quickly may render the information permanently unavailable.

■ Cell phones can be purchased with prepaid minutes, maintaining the user's anonymity.

■ Data, particularly voice mail and e-mail held by a service provider, may be remotely purged. Consider a preservation order under 18 U.S.C. § 2703(f).

■ The technical capabilities of cell phones (e.g., the push-to-talk feature) are constantly changing. Contact the service provider for the most up-to-date information related to current capabilities of the device and service provided.

■ Some cell phones use **Subscriber Identity Module (SIM)** cards to store their identifying information. Criminals may exchange SIM cards within one phone or use numerous SIM cards among more than one phone to conceal identity or thwart investigations.

■ When seizing cell phones, remember the following:

— Data can be lost if the battery dies.

— Keypad-locked passwords, which are activated when the cell phones are turned off, can be difficult to defeat.

— Phones left on should be protected from radio frequency (RF) signals by placing them in a container that blocks these signals (e.g., **Faraday cage,** clean metal paint can). Be aware that in doing so, the battery may drain faster because it will continue to search for a signal.

— Prior to powering off the phone, determine if specialists should be consulted and contact them for procedural guidance.

— Specialists or retail manufacturers may be able to obtain more data.

STOP All **Bluetooth**®-enabled devices being used by law enforcement should be turned off prior to entering a search scene because wireless synchronization may occur with media located at the scene.

Legal considerations

■ Seizing or searching cell phones implicates Fourth Amendment concerns.

■ Obtaining information, including voice mail, from a service provider will raise ECPA or State-specific issues pertaining to the recovery of electronic data. Consider sending a preservation letter under 18 U.S.C. § 2703(f) to a provider.

■ With a Title III wiretap order (or State equivalent), law enforcement may intercept the content of mobile communication devices (to include instant messaging, numeric pages, voice communication, etc.).

■ Legal process may be needed to obtain the data described above.

Refer to Chapter 3, Legal Issues, for additional information.

Scenarios

1. A victim is abducted and placed in the trunk of a car. The victim makes a telephone call from her cell phone, and triangulation of the signal identifies her physical location, leading to her rescue.

2. A homicide occurs on the east side of a city. The primary suspect's alibi is refuted by the data (cell site records) that establishes the physical location of the suspect's cell phone at the time of the murder.

3. A complaint comes in to the police station pertaining to a suspicious person at the public pool. A law enforcement officer responds and conducts a field interview of the person. The officer discovers the person has a cell phone with a built-in camera. The officer determines the person has been taking pictures of children changing in the locker room.

Computers (desktops and laptops)

Traditional

Ice Cube: Small personal computer
with carry handle

Introduction

A computer is a general purpose machine that processes data according to a set of instructions.

Value of computers

- Investigators can use these to do the following:

  — Perform various functions such as conducting research, analyzing and organizing data, managing cases, and performing financial analyses.

  — Access a subject's computer, which may reveal data useful to an investigation, such as disclosing the subject's activities (e.g., sent e-mails), or the identity of criminal associates or additional victims.

  — Communicate with suspects during undercover operations (e.g., Internet predator investigations).

- Subjects can additionally use these for the following:

  — To store data such as records, photographs, stolen information, and e-mails (container).

  — To commit numerous criminal acts, such as creating forged IDs, conducting research, cyberstalking, and communicating over the Internet (tool).

  — As targets of theft (fruit of the crime).

  — As targets of the crime (e.g., intrusion, denial of service attack).

Identifying and obtaining computers

- Personal computers are commercially available and may be purchased as either a complete system or individual components.

- Personal computers are generally easily identified, but technological advances and user expertise may change their appearance and make them less readily recognizable.

- PDAs can perform the same functions as computers; the line between personal computers and PDAs is quickly blurring.

Special investigatory and other considerations

- Data may be stored internally or on separate or remote storage media (see section on removable storage media and players).

- When seizing a computer found in the off position, leave it off. Powering up a computer may alter data.

- When seizing a computer that is found running, photograph and document the data on the screen. If expert assistance is not available to help with powering down the system, unplugging the computer is the preferable method for powering the system down, although this may result in the loss of information. For more information see the United States Secret Service (USSS) *Best Practices for Seizing Electronic Evidence, Version 2* (www.fletc.gov/legal/downloads/bestpractices.pdf)

 Review the section on volatility of digital evidence in chapter 1.

- Data on a computer connected to a network or the Internet (via cable or wireless) may be remotely accessed, deleted, or altered. Protecting this data may require isolating it from networks or the Internet.

- Isolating the computer will not secure data stored on networks or the Internet. Additional legal process may be required to preserve and seize this information.

Legal considerations

- Searching and seizing computers and their data implicate the Fourth Amendment. For more information, see Chapter 3, Legal Issues.

Scenarios

1. In an attempt to locate a fugitive, a search of a relative's computer discloses e-mails and letters to the fugitive. Further, searching Web history reveals the use of online mapping tools (www.mapquest.com). These two pieces of information help locate the fugitive.

2. Investigators are uncertain whether a victim died as a result of a homicide or a suicide. Search of the victim's computer reveals a *blog* indicating the victim's depression and suicidal ideation.

3. During a homicide investigation, examination of a suspect's computer reveals numerous visits to Web sites consistent with planning the crime (e.g., instructions for poisons, bombs, and how to not get caught).

4. During a traffic stop, the officer observes a large amount of card stock, preprinted barcodes, a laptop computer, and retail goods. Subsequent investigation reveals a

suspect engaged in barcode forgery, manufacturing fraudulent barcodes to purchase consumer goods at a significant discount. A forensic examination of the laptop computer revealed barcode images and driver's license templates, which were used to facilitate the return of the retail items at their original prices.

Credit card fraud devices

Three-track reader: Reads and records multiple tracks on a magnetic stripe from a single card (e g , credit cards, magnetically encoded driver's licenses, health care cards, password entry, fitness club cards).

Skimmer/Reader: Handheld, records information off any credit card. Holds information from hundreds of credit cards and can be connected to a computer for transfer and use.

Skimmer/Reader: Attached directly to a PDA to enable immediate usage.

Point-of-sale authorizer: Used to authorize credit cards.

Introduction

Some of these are legitimate devices used for illicit purposes. In some jurisdictions, mere possession of these devices is illegal. The devices can be divided into four general categories:

- Skimmers capture credit card information contained on the magnetic data stripe on plastic cards, such as number, expiration date, and owner information (e.g., name, address).

- *Encoders* write fraudulent information on credit cards, blank card stock, driver's licenses, or any other device bearing a magnetic data stripe and/or a chip.

- *Three-track readers* allow users to decode and verify data from all three tracks of the magnetic data stripe on the credit card. In the United States, tracks 1 and 2 on a magnetic data stripe are used to hold account information. Track 3 may be used by the card issuer to hold discretionary information on the cardholder.

- Point-of-sale authorizers record transactions at the checkout area in a retail store and also are used to check credit limits.

Note: The above devices also can be used to create access-control devices or to encode information on magnetic stripes embedded within counterfeit documents. Data associated with the device are stored either on the device (if standalone) or on the computer(s) to which the device is attached.

Value of the credit card fraud device

- Investigators should note the following:

  — Possession or use of the device may be evidence that a subject is involved in identity theft, credit card fraud, or other fraudulent activity.

  — Data stored within these devices can be used to generate timelines and historical activity.

- Subjects may do the following:

  — Possess a device while working at a retail outlet and use it to capture customer information. Customer information can either be used by the offender or sold to a third party to commit identity theft.

  — Possess a device to encode stolen or fraudulent information on counterfeit credit cards or other counterfeit documents possessing magnetic stripes.

Identifying and obtaining the credit card fraud device

- Credit card skimmers and encoders can be handheld and look like a standard credit card reader. They may be attached to a computer or PDA to download data (e.g., credit card numbers and other account information).

- A skimmer may look like a small square device similar to a pager, with a track for swiping a credit card.

- Point-of-sale devices can be found on or near persons working with credit cards and on or near computers.

  — Some legitimate devices can be used for illegitimate purposes. For example, a hotel room key encoder can be used to capture information from a guest's credit card. This data can then be encoded onto a blank credit card or any card bearing a magnetic stripe.

- These devices are commercially available or can be fabricated.

Special investigatory and other considerations

- Information relating to the use of the device could be found on other storage media seized in the investigation (e.g., information collected by a skimmer could be downloaded to a PDA or computer).

- A large volume of blank magnetic stripe cards could indicate fraudulent or illegal intent. A credit card reader should be used to analyze any data contained within these cards.

Legal considerations

Law enforcement searches of these devices usually implicate Fourth Amendment concerns. For more information, see Chapter 3, Legal Issues.

Scenario

A credit card company analyzing fraudulent charges identifies a restaurant as the common point of compromise for numerous customers' credit cards. During the investigation, the investigator observes one waiter with a small black device that the waiter is using to skim credit card information when processing transactions. When the skimmer is analyzed, it is found to contain hundreds of stored credit card numbers.

Customer or user cards and devices

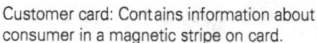

Transponder: Holds account and authorization information pertaining to a consumer and is specific to the corporation that accepts it (e.g., Speedpass™).

Customer card: Contains information about consumer in a magnetic stripe on card.

Introduction

This section addresses various cards and other devices used by consumers that contain data on a magnetic stripe, embedded chip, holograms, one- or two-dimensional barcodes, RF devices, or other storage technologies. These cards include credit cards, restaurant cards, customer reward cards, mileage cards, club cards, and driver's licenses.

Data associated with the card are either stored on the card itself or maintained at a centralized database located at the company that issues the card or services the account. The data contained depend on the issuing entity. Some examples of traceable data include purchase history, customer name, address, telephone number, status for that organization, and biometric data. The cards are generally swiped during a transaction or other event that necessitates updating the data contained on the card or database.

Value of customer or user cards

- Investigators can use these to do the following:

  — Analyze the data on the card, which may provide investigative leads. Transaction records may help an investigator identify the subject's location, movement, or other actions (e.g., use of a phone card to make threatening calls may allow investigators to identify the caller, call recipient, times of calls, and location of caller).

  — Analyze a subject's spending habits through card activity, which may show spending beyond legitimate income and suggest the possibility of unlawful proceeds. Cards to consider include supermarket cards, casino loyalty cards, and credit cards.

- Subjects can additionally use these to do the following:

  — Engage in fraud, theft, identity theft, or similar crimes.

  — Create false alibis by allowing accomplices to use their cards.

Identifying and obtaining customer or user cards and devices

- These devices can be incorporated into credit cards, key chain cards, and electronic transmission devices (key chain fobs).

- The cards may be lawfully obtained from the issuing entity, obtained from the issuing entity through fraud (using a pseudonym or other illegitimate identity), stolen, or created by subjects.

Special investigatory and other considerations

- Data maintained by the card issuer may be used to establish the movement of the card and determine how it was used.

- As technology advances, the form and use of these cards may change. Investigators should take special notice of any devices with which they are not familiar.

Legal considerations

- Law enforcement searches of these devices possessed by an individual will implicate Fourth Amendment concerns.

- Access to the card does not necessarily give law enforcement access to any remotely stored data. State or Federal privacy laws may limit law enforcement access to records possessed by businesses or card issuers.

- For more information, see Chapter 3, Legal Issues.

Scenario

During a possible suicide investigation, a single red rose and a typed suicide note are found next to the decedent. The decedent's wife comments that he was depressed and does not know where he purchased the flower. A review of the wife's customer user card for a local supermarket reveals that she herself purchased a rose on the day of her husband's death. Further forensic examination of the wife's computer reveals that the suicide note was written after the time of death.

Data preservation (duplicating, imaging, copying)

Drive duplicator   Forensic drive duplicator

Introduction

Data preservation tools are hardware, *firmware,* or software (or a combination) that allow for an accurate duplicate of all data contained on a digital storage device (e.g., hard drive, CD-ROM, flash memory, floppy disk, *Zip®, Jaz®*). The source system can be a computer, PDA, cell phone, or other electronic device. Duplication tools are used to acquire entire pieces of media. In some cases, copying selected files may also be satisfactory.

The three general methods for data preservation are as follows:

- A duplicate copy of all data from one physical device to another device is commonly referred to as a clone. This results in two devices with identical information.

- A duplicate copy of all data from a physical device to a file or set of files is commonly referred to as an image. This file is generally used as a transfer medium and for storage.

- A logical copy is created by copying only the files from one piece of media to another. This process does not capture all available data on the original device (e.g., deleted data).

STOP When using software imaging tools, *write protection* and image authentication should be considered.

Value of imaging

- To investigators:

  — Law enforcement uses imaging to gather and preserve data from computers or electronic devices. Examples of such data are the following:

- Documents, spreadsheets, e-mails, instant messaging, or other evidence of criminal activities.

- Deleted files. Note that many computer users think that deleting a file actually eliminates the information. However, depending on how the files are deleted, forensic computer examiners may be able to recover all or part of the original data.

- Intellectual property (e.g., copyright violations).

- Contraband, such as the following:

  - Child pornography.

  - Counterfeit currency.

  - Stolen credit card numbers.

- Evidence that an electronic device was used in the commission of offenses, such as the following:

  - Fraud.

  - Stalking.

  - Child enticement.

— When a system is copied, the output can be a true copy of the contents of one device placed onto another. In some instances this process is commonly referred to as cloning. Examples:

- Disk to disk.

- Cell phone to cell phone.

— When a system is imaged, the output file(s) can be used for the following:

- Archiving (evidence preservation).

- Transfer and restoration to another device or media.

- Analysis.

— The use of traditional imaging tools and techniques may not be necessary to copy selected files *(logical file copy)*.

— None of the activities in this section should be attempted without training.

Note: Refer to the NIJ publication *Forensic Examination of Digital Evidence: A Guide for Law Enforcement* (www.ojp.usdoj.gov/nij/pubs-sum/199408.htm).

- To subjects:

  — Subjects' possession of imaging tools may be lawful but their use may not be.

  — Subjects may use imaging hardware and software to backup, transfer, and restore their data.

Identifying and obtaining the imaging tool

- Imaging tools can be lawfully obtained through software and hardware vendors. Distribution of some products is restricted to law enforcement.

- The presence of imaging software, software manuals, or associated hardware (such as write blockers, data transfer cables, or hardware keys) will indicate that subjects may be using imaging tools.

Special investigatory and other considerations

- Sharing an image with other parties may require multiple copies of software (and the correct version) or device.

- Some data itself may be contraband. However, an image may need to be shared in the following circumstances:

  — Pursuant to a discovery order.

  — In joint investigations or task forces.

  — To coordinate cases with prosecutors.

- Consider the unique issues associated with large images or numbers of devices to be imaged, such as the following:

  — Shelf life of storage media.

  — Cost of the storage media.

  — Physical storage requirements.

  — Time required for onsite imaging.

  — Time required for analysis.

- Consider officer safety and environmental concerns at the location where devices are imaged. This may require removing the device to be imaged to another location.

- Imaging at the scene may be necessary when seizure of the original is not practical or possible. Examples:

  — Intrusiveness or economic impact of seizing the hardware itself.

  — Court orders or warrants preventing hardware seizure.

— Agency resource limitations to store seized hardware.

— Duplicates or images also allow for working copies while preserving the original.

Legal considerations

Legal considerations are rare in using imaging tools provided the user has lawful access to the device and information being imaged.

To obtain lawful access, law enforcement will use traditional Fourth Amendment tools such as the following:

- Consent, which also includes banners or signed user agreements.

- Search warrants.

- Subpoenas.

- Other legal process.

Some special considerations in drafting search warrants to gain access to information that law enforcement wants to image are the following:

- The need to describe the search strategy in the warrant.

- The need to justify the seizure of the original device to be imaged.

- The need to describe with particularity the type of information investigators wish to seize.

Note: The U.S. Department of Justice publishes and keeps current a manual on *Searching and Seizing Computers and Obtaining Electronic Evidence in Criminal Investigations* at www.cybercrime.gov. This resource also contains "go-bys" for obtaining legal access to the device and information to be imaged.

Scenarios

1. In a major bid-rigging case, the corporate defendant denies having knowledge of competitors' bids for a new stadium prior to submitting its bid. Agents execute a search warrant on the corporation's computers and forensically image all of the media, preserving the data to include files the corporate officers thought they had deleted. After analyzing preserved data, the prosecution is able to prove the corporate officers had prior knowledge of competitors' bids.

2. A suspect in a child pornography investigation learns that police have executed a search warrant at the home of a child pornography trading partner. Prior to officers executing a search warrant at the suspect's residence, the suspect reformats his computer hard drive. Police seize the computer and image the suspect's drive. Forensic tools are used to successfully recover images of child pornography.

Detection and interception (wireless)

Air magnet: Network interception and detection device used to monitor networks, wireless communication, and all associated network activity.

Cantenna: An inexpensive wireless version of a long-range antenna used to extend the range of a wireless network or detect or intercept other wireless networks.

Improvised antenna for the purpose of detecting wireless networks.

Mobile antenna hidden in a backpack for the purpose of detecting wireless network.

WiFi Detector: Wireless network signal locator and strength detector.

Introduction

A variety of devices and associated programs are designed to locate or intercept wireless communication from phones or computer networks. This section will only address detecting the presence of a network, not the interception of the communications themselves. Refer to the section on sniffers later in this chapter and Chapter 3, Legal Issues, for more information.

Value of detection devices

- To investigators:

  — Investigators may be able to detect, identify, or rule out the use of wireless devices.

- To subjects:

  — Subjects may be able to detect the presence of wireless devices or access points for the purpose of unauthorized access.

  — When investigators use wireless transmitters (e.g., wireless bugs), subjects may detect their presence.

  — Subjects may intercept wireless communications (eavesdropping) to steal information or conduct other criminal activity.

Identifying and obtaining detection devices

- Detection devices may be standalone handheld items that can detect the presence of a wireless network.

- Wireless communication devices, such as wireless enabled PDAs and computers, can also detect a wireless network. For example, properly configured, Windows® **operating systems** will automatically scan for the presence of a wireless network.

- Examples of hardware wireless detection devices include air magnets, baby monitors, shortwave radios, and scanners.

- Examples of software used to detect wireless networks include Kismet, AirSnort, NetStumbler. Keep in mind that these software applications are capable of intercepting wireless network traffic.

Special investigatory and other considerations

- Law enforcement should be aware of individuals sitting in a parking lot with a laptop computer using a directional antenna **(wardriving).** They may be attempting to illegally access a wireless network.

- Law enforcement devices with wireless connectivity capability may be subject to detection.

Legal considerations

- There are generally no prohibitions against an individual or law enforcement detecting the presence of a wireless network.

- Accessing a network may require a subscription or other permissions. Unauthorized access may violate State or Federal laws.

■ Intercepting the contents of communications over a wireless network implicates the Fourth Amendment and Title III.

For more information, see Chapter 3, Legal Issues.

Scenarios

1. An offender was illegally accessing the wireless hotspot of a local business in an effort to obtain anonymous Internet access. In an effort to identify the offender, officers incrementally turned down the signal strength of the wireless network. This allowed them to observe that someone was moving closer and closer to the building from the parking lot, leading to the apprehension of the offender.

2. Officers have a search warrant to seize "all computers and PDAs" at a particular location. During the execution of the search a wireless access point is discovered through the use of a wireless detector; however, no wireless devices or computers have been found. Officers continue to search and find wireless devices hidden in the attic rafters, where they may not have ordinarily searched. One of the devices recovered from the rafters is the device on which the evidence to convict is discovered.

3. A man has given a lava lamp to a young girl who babysits for his children. He has installed a pinhole webcam in the lava lamp. The man goes online, representing himself as a teenage boy, and persuades the girl to masturbate in her bedroom. The images of her are projected to his house next door. A neighbor's video baby monitor happens to pick up the girl's activity and the incident is reported to the police. The man is identified and is successfully prosecuted.

Digital cameras and Web cameras

Camera lighter: Digital camera incorporated into the body of a lighter. Features include high-resolution digital still camera with internal memory, a surveillance feature that records images at preset time intervals, and video recording with sound.

Webcam: Camera that interfaces with a computer to transfer live images.

Camera phone

Introduction

Digital cameras are increasingly used in place of traditional film cameras. Additionally, they are being incorporated into many other consumer products such as cell phones. Digital cameras capture images in digital format so they can be electronically transmitted, stored, or altered. Digital and Web cameras are smaller than most film cameras and can be concealed for covert use. Web cameras are a special type of digital camera, and are used in conjunction with a computer either by a cable or wireless connection. Such devices may take either still or video images and, if a microphone is integrated, may also capture sound.

Value of digital and Web cameras

- To investigators:

  — These cameras can be used for surveillance, documentation during searches, or other operations in which a film camera could be used.

  — Digital cameras provide immediate images (versus film developing time). Portable printers can print digital images onsite for quick distribution.

  — Digital cameras may allow for the recording of voice notes to accompany the images.

  — Digital images allow for real-time distribution to multiple destinations.

- To subjects:

  — Subjects use digital cameras for all the purposes for which a film camera would be used.

  — These cameras are especially prevalent in child exploitation crimes, covert surveillance, counterfeiting, and identity theft.

Identifying and obtaining digital and Web cameras

- Digital cameras can be found in, or integrated with, any sort of electronic/computing device. Cell phones or other concealed cameras (e.g., camera concealed in a lighter "007 lighter") in particular can be used to take pictures without the subject's knowledge.

- Media for these devices can be removable or integrated into the device through a variety of memory storage devices (e.g., computers, microdrives, or floppy disks).

Special investigatory and other considerations

- The data captured or stored with digital cameras consist of pictures, video, or sound. Even if these data have been deleted from the device, it may be recoverable in some circumstances.

- Most digital cameras embed information in the image files of photographs. This information, called **metadata,** can include serial number, make and model of the camera, lens and lighting information, and date and time settings and may have to be accessed with special software.

■ As with all electronic devices, date and time settings can be manipulated by the user.

■ If a digital camera is seized, submit the camera for forensic examination.

Legal considerations

■ Fourth Amendment considerations apply when seizing or searching digital cameras or related storage devices.

■ Fourth Amendment considerations apply when law enforcement uses digital cameras in areas where there are reasonable expectations of privacy.

■ When audio is captured, Title III considerations may apply.

See Chapter 3, Legal Issues, for more information.

Scenarios

1. Crime scene investigators are processing a location in a remote area. A latent fingerprint is processed and photographed with a digital camera. This image is e-mailed to the crime lab from the scene. The crime lab processes the print through the Automated Fingerprint Identification System (AFIS) and obtains a cold hit in 15 minutes.

2. An AMBER Alert comes in for a missing child and officers immediately need a photograph to be used on fliers. Officers obtain a digital photograph from the missing child's parents and produce fliers immediately and e-mail the photograph to neighboring jurisdictions and the media. The jurisdictions with mobile data terminals send the photo to all the terminals, showing the missing person.

Digital security cameras

Introduction

Digital security cameras are used to record still images or video, with or without audio. Recording functions may include time lapse, real time, **multiplex,** and motion activated.

Value of digital security cameras

- To investigators:

  — The data collected by digital security cameras can assist in documenting the who, what, where, and when of a crime.

- To subjects:

  — Subjects may use digital security cameras for surveillance and to commit crimes involving stalking or voyeurism.

Identifying and obtaining digital security cameras and systems

- Digital security cameras and systems are normally affixed to property in public areas such as on an ATM, in high-crime areas on high poles, at traffic and toll booths, and in banks and retail establishments for security and loss-prevention purposes. Increasingly, these cameras are found in or on residences and daycare facilities.

- These cameras may be obvious, such as bank cameras, or hidden, as in a casino or for loss-prevention purposes.

Special investigatory and other considerations

- The data collected by these systems may be stored on the camera itself (e.g., tape, CD, DVD, or other digital media) or on a remote computer. The data may be transferred or transmitted from the camera to the computer by wire or wireless means.

- The information from these cameras may be stored in proprietary formats and specialized hardware or software may be required to access it.

- Digital evidence should be saved in its highest quality and resolution format. Some video formats compress data, resulting in a loss of detail.

- Enhancement of video surveillance recordings may be accomplished with commonly used hardware and software. For example, the use of a projector can visually enlarge an image to make details of the image more visible. Commercial viewing software has stop-motion or time-lapsed capabilities.

Legal considerations

- Video-only cameras installed in public areas, or areas where there is no reasonable expectation of privacy, usually do not implicate Fourth Amendment concerns.

- Use of video-only cameras in areas where there is a reasonable expectation of privacy may require a search warrant or consent of a person who is present during the recording. These systems and those that also record audio may violate State privacy laws or implicate Title III.

■ Digital images can be compromised by a variety of means. Forensic procedures for the handling and processing of digital evidence should be followed to ensure the security and authenticity of the data.

See Chapter 3, Legal Issues, for more information.

Scenario

Following a child abduction in a parking lot, the area is canvassed for security cameras. The security camera from a store is determined to have captured the crime on tape and leads to the identification of the abductor.

Encryption tools and passphrase protection

Introduction

Encryption tools are hardware or software based, or a combination of both, that protect data by rendering the data inaccessible without use of one or more of the following: a password, a passphrase, a "software **key,**" or a physical access device.

■ Encryption tools that can be employed on physical devices include **dongles,** key cards, and biometric devices.

■ Tools that are features of the media itself include the following:

— Integrated drive or device electronics linked to a specific motherboard.

— Encryption built into the disk that automatically encrypts data.

— BIOS or boot passphrases.

■ Encryption can be an integral feature of the operating system (e.g., Microsoft® **Encrypted File System (EFS)).**

■ Encryption tools can be standalone software (e.g., **Pretty Good Privacy (PGP),** WinZip®). In addition, these tools may be a feature of common application software (e.g., Microsoft®Word, Excel, accounting packages).

■ Software-based **decryption tools** may have the capability to reveal, disable, or bypass passphrases. These passphrases, however, may not be the actual ones used by the subject(s).

Value of encryption tools

■ To investigators:

— Law enforcement uses encryption to protect data, such as reports, documents, spreadsheets, e-mails, instant messaging logs, or other sensitive information, including evidence.

— Decryption by law enforcement may be necessary to do the following:

- Recover evidence.

- Show intent on the part of the suspect to hide evidence.

■ To subjects:

— Criminals may use encryption to prevent the discovery by law enforcement of contraband or evidence such as the following:

- Child pornography.

- Counterfeit currency details.

- Stolen credit card numbers.

- E-mail or chat files.

- Intellectual property information.

— Corporations use encryption tools to do the following:

- Protect against theft of intellectual property.

- Secure or protect data (e.g., client data) from unauthorized access either by network intrusion or theft of hardware.

Identifying and obtaining encryption tools

■ Encryption tools can be obtained through software and hardware vendors.

■ Possession of encryption tools may be lawful but their use may not be (e.g., a subject might encrypt his employer's data to deny access to the data).

■ Law enforcement may know whether subjects are using encryption tools when they locate encryption software, software manuals, or associated hardware (e.g., dongles).

Special investigatory and other considerations

■ Detection of encryption at the scene may compel the following:

— Require the seizure of the original hardware and the accurate documentation (e.g., photograph, diagram, and label connections) of the original configuration.

— Require contacting an expert to seize the data safely. Although shutting down the system and seizing the hardware may be the only available option, the investigator should be aware that this may result in the permanent loss of encrypted data. A forensics expert may be able to provide guidance on this issue.

— Necessitate requests for passphrases from the following:

- System administrators.

- Coworkers.

- Assistants.

- Subjects.

— Be a basis to obtain a wiretap to learn the subject's passphrase.

■ Knowledge that the subject uses encryption may require a more detailed search at the site for the following:

— Passphrases (look under the keyboard, under the monitor, in software manuals, in notes, etc.).

— Information relating to authors of the encryption program to determine decryption possibilities.

— Personal information about the subject that may reveal passphrases (e.g., family name, pet name, anniversary).

■ In addition:

— Encryption algorithms can be implemented to a varying degree of complexity. The stronger encryption packages are virtually unbreakable with current techniques.

— Obtaining the passphrase from the subject or through a thorough search at the scene may be the only means of decryption.

— Some jurisdictions permit using legal process to compel the production of a physical access device (e.g., biometrics).

Legal considerations

There are rarely legal considerations in using decryption tools provided the user has lawful access to the device and information being decrypted.

Note: If a person consents to the search of media but does not know the passphrase, the person may not have authority to consent to a search of the encrypted media. The scope of a search warrant should include the ability to search for and seize relevant password and other access information not residing on the computer itself.

Scenarios

1. Law enforcement agencies are sharing information with other agencies. Though not classified, this information is sensitive. This information is encrypted to ensure that it cannot be read by unauthorized recipients.

2. The parties to a conspiracy use PGP to encrypt all e-mail correspondence. A law enforcement forensics examiner was able to recover the PGP passphrase from one of the individual's computers and decrypt all of the e-mail traffic.

3. A forensics examiner was able to reveal a passphrase masked by symbols (*****) in a password entry screen or **dialog box** using appropriate software.

Facsimile (fax)

Fax-enabled phone   External fax modem

Introduction

Fax machines provide the ability to transmit and receive copies of documents. Many fax machines are also capable of making document copies. Standalone fax machines must have the hard copy original fed into them and are connected to a phone line. Computers with fax capability can send faxes to traditional fax machines as well as other computers.

Fax machines have evolved into multipurpose machines capable of providing such services as faxing, copying, and scanning, and may have internal storage capabilities.

Value of fax machines

- To investigators:

  — Data related to crimes may be found stored in fax machine memory, such as the contents of recently faxed documents and stored telephone numbers of other fax machines.

- To subjects:

  — Fax machines may be used by subjects to conduct criminal activities, including fraud, **spamming,** and the communication of threats.

  — The automatic redial function may be used for harassment or stalking.

Identifying and obtaining fax machines

■ Standalone fax machines look like small printers with a telephone keypad. The fax capability can be integrated into a computer or multifunction machines that also print, copy, or scan.

■ Standalone fax machines are connected to telephone lines.

Special investigatory and other considerations

■ Sending party information is often included in a fax transmission, but it may be altered by the sending party and therefore may be inaccurate.

■ Some fax machines retain logs of outbound or inbound faxes.

■ If the fax device is not computer based, information can be stored in internal memory, which can retain hundreds of pages. Older model fax machines have film cartridges from which one may be able to read old faxes.

■ If a computer is used to send a fax, the data sent or received may be on the hard drive (i.e., no fax machine will be recovered). Any such computer should be seized and examined. Data may be remotely purged from computer-based fax devices.

■ Faxes have limited and *volatile memory.*

— Data contained on fax devices is perishable and may be lost if power is interrupted.

— Consider unplugging the telephone line to prevent the receipt of further faxes that may overwrite existing data.

Legal considerations

■ Intercepting a fax between points of transmission requires a wiretap order.

■ Legal process is required to obtain information that is remotely stored with a Web-based fax service.

■ Traditional Fourth Amendment rules apply to received faxes and information stored within the device.

See Chapter 3, Legal Issues, for more information.

Global positioning system devices

Handheld GPS   GPS watches

Introduction

Global positioning system (GPS) receivers, in conjunction with GPS satellites, identify the location of persons, vehicles, or items that contain the receiver. Data collected from GPS receivers can permit tracking of persons or items. Some GPS devices are integrated with mapping software.

Value of GPS

- To investigators:

  — GPS receivers allow officers to pinpoint their own locations for such purposes as the following:

    ▪ Mapping a crime scene.

    ▪ Describing a search warrant location.

    ▪ Officer safety.

    ▪ Logging moving surveillance activities.

    ▪ GPS receivers and transmitter combinations may be used to track vehicles, objects, or persons. Depending on the technology used, the tracking information may be stored on a device or transmitted to a monitoring device.

    ▪ A suspect's GPS device may reveal historical information regarding movement, speed, and stored **waypoints.**

- To subjects:

  — GPS can be used by subjects in manners similar to law enforcement.

  — GPS allows subjects to do the following:

    ▪ Plan routes.

    ▪ Track shipments.

    ▪ Pinpoint locations, people, or objects.

Identifying and obtaining GPS devices

- GPS devices are commercially available.

- GPS devices can be permanently mounted, handheld, or covert.

- GPS capability may be integrated into cell phones, PDAs, vehicles (e.g., OnStar®), and almost any other electronic device.

Special investigatory and other considerations

- Handheld GPS receivers store data within the device or on accompanying media.

- When GPS information is transmitted, data could be located on the device itself or with the service provider (e.g., OnStar®, cellular phone companies).

Legal considerations

- Installing a GPS device where there is no reasonable expectation of privacy does not implicate the Fourth Amendment. Some State statutes, however, require legal process.

- Installing a GPS device where there is a reasonable expectation of privacy (such as entering the curtilage of a residence, entering a private automobile, or opening a package) implicates the Fourth Amendment, and legal authority is usually required.

- Tracking the GPS device in an area where there is no reasonable expectation of privacy does not implicate the Fourth Amendment, but some States and Federal circuit courts have statutes or decisions that require legal authority to accomplish such tracking.

- Tracking the GPS device when the device moves to a location where there is a reasonable expectation of privacy implicates the Fourth Amendment, and legal authority is required.

- These considerations vary among jurisdictions and may be subject to more stringent regulations than listed. Consult legal counsel for direction.

Scenarios

1. A salesman in California is suspected of murdering his wife. A covertly installed GPS device reveals that he has since parked his vehicle within 1 mile of the remote location at which his wife's body is ultimately discovered.

2. A suspect is believed to have murdered his daughter and buried her. A GPS device is installed in his vehicle and determines that he visits one location in the woods for 45 minutes, another location for about 15 minutes, then returns to the first location for about 10 minutes. Going to these two locations, officers find the victim buried in one location and trace evidence that she had previously been buried in the other location. Officers are able to demonstrate the offender went to the first location to dig a grave, the second to exhume and remove the hastily buried victim, and returned to the pre-dug grave to rebury the child.

3. A passenger is thrown from a boat and dies. Witnesses observed the boat racing at high speed just prior to the incident. The boat had a GPS unit installed which, when analyzed, revealed the boat speed at the time of the accident was in excess of 100 miles per hour.

4. In the course of executing a search warrant on a suspected drug dealer, officers discover a handheld GPS unit. Examination of the unit reveals several waypoints that lead to the discovery of drug caches.

5. A woman who has a protective order against her estranged husband takes her car in for service. The mechanic discovers a GPS receiver attached to the underside of the vehicle. Further investigation reveals the GPS receiver was placed on the car by the woman's husband, who was stalking her.

Home entertainment

Front and back view of home theater system

TiVo®

Xbox® gaming console

Introduction

Home entertainment devices exist that investigators should be aware of because they may contain information relevant to investigations, such as the following:

■ TiVo®. TiVo service uses a digital video recorder (similar to a VCR but with a hard drive) to record up to 80 hours of television. The TiVo® console can be modified to store electronic information unrelated to recorded television programs. (See Appendix C, Hacked Devices, for more information.)

■ Game consoles. Game consoles (e.g., Xbox®, PlayStation®, Nintendo®) are used to play video games. Many game consoles come with internal hard drives and are capable of Internet connectivity. Video game consoles can be modified to store electronic information. (See Appendix C, Hacked Devices, for more information.)

- Cable and satellite access devices. These devices allow the user access to cable and satellite programming services. They may store information relating to the viewing history of the subscriber. These devices can be altered to allow unauthorized access to premium channels.

- WebTV. A device used to access the Internet. Older *WebTV* devices do not have hard drives, newer ones do.

Value of home entertainment devices

- To investigators:

  — Video recording devices may contain evidence of crimes such as child pornography or subjects' films of their own criminal activities.

  — The presence of large numbers of these devices may be evidence of copyright piracy or unauthorized access to subscription services like cable TV.

  — Examination of these devices can be used to establish theft of the device itself or of unauthorized access to subscription service.

  — The device may archive viewing histories that can be used to establish timelines or to confirm or refute alibis. For subscriber-based devices, the service provider may maintain additional records.

- To subjects:

  — Depending on the nature of the device, it may be used to steal proprietary information, obtain unauthorized access to subscription services, or to store evidence of criminal activity.

Identifying and obtaining home entertainment devices

- These items are commercially available.

- Methods and components to modify these products can be obtained from the Internet.

Special investigatory and other considerations

- Because the majority of these items are associated with televisions, when they are not connected to a television, illicit use should be suspected.

- Examine the device for signs of physical tampering as evidence of modification, which may yield probative information.

- Specific crimes may have special considerations. See Appendix C, Hacked Devices, for more information.

Legal considerations

- Fourth Amendment considerations apply for seizure and searches of these devices.

- Requesting customer subscription information from a video cable or satellite provider regarding viewing history will require compliance with the Cable Act, 47 U.S.C. § 551. This statute requires that the investigator give prior notice to subjects that they are targets of an investigation.

- Requesting customer records from a cable or satellite service provider regarding Internet service requires compliance with ECPA.

See Chapter 3, Legal Issues, for more information.

Scenario

A suspect indicates that he was at home watching a particular television program during the time of the crime under investigation. However, a review of the stored records in the suspect's satellite system disprove his statement.

Internet tools

Introduction

The Internet provides a rich source of information that is available 24 hours a day. Most of this information is free, although not all information obtained may be accurate. The most common Internet tools include Web browsers (e.g., Internet Explorer®, Netscape®) and search engines (e.g., Google™, Yahoo!®, Ask Jeeves®).

For additional information on the use of the tools highlighted in this section, refer to *Investigations Involving the Internet and Computer Networks* (www.ojp.usdoj.gov/nij/pubs-sum/210798.htm).

Value of Internet tools

- To investigators:

  — The amount and types of information available on the Internet are unlimited. For example, the Internet can provide the following:

    - Personal information (e.g., names, telephone numbers, addresses).

    - Financial data. (May require access to commercial databases for a fee.)

    - Maps.

    - Public records, to include court filings.

    - Legal research (e.g., cases, statutes, policies).

    - Technical information.

- To subjects:

  — Subjects can use the Internet the same way as law enforcement and are able to obtain the same information.

  — Subjects also use the Internet to obtain information to select victims or to steal and use private information (e.g., credit card numbers). The Internet is a prime source of information used in identity theft.

  — The Internet may be the mechanism that subjects use to commit various crimes, most notably frauds, identity theft, and child exploitation.

Identifying and obtaining Internet tools

- Many Internet sites are dedicated to providing extensive lists of research sites that are useful to investigators. For example, searching Google™ (www.google.com) with the keywords "Maryland real property" can provide information on accessing the State Department of Assessment and Taxation (SDAT) site and various public records.

Special investigatory and other considerations

- It is not uncommon for some sites on the Internet to contain inaccurate information. Consider the reliability of the source when determining the accuracy of the information.

- Access to the Internet is affordable for any department. Any location with a computer and a telephone or cable connection can have Internet access. Most metropolitan areas have high-speed access.

STOP Law enforcement must take special precautions when using the Internet in an undercover role. E-mails contain encoded information that can reveal the identity of the sender or the computer the sender used. Visiting a Web site may leave behind this same coded information revealing who (or what computer) visited the Web site. Computers and identities used in undercover operations should not be attributable to an agency network or individual.

Legal considerations

Possession of information gained by the use of certain tools may violate privacy statutes (e.g., obtaining credit card information from a Web database).

Scenarios

1. Local county government offices often have property descriptions and photographs of properties online. Online research of these descriptions can be useful for search warrant attachments or preraid briefings.

2. Investigators use an Internet search engine to locate, download, and print an operating manual for a piece of equipment seized in an investigation.

Internet tools to identify users and Internet connections (investigative)

Overview

The ability to identify **domain names,** Internet Protocol (IP) addresses, and the owners of IP addresses and domain names is an integral part of conducting Internet investigations. Determining how a suspect's computer is connected to the Internet, and how data are routed, can also provide valuable information. The most common utilities to accomplish these investigatory goals, explained on subsequent pages, are the following:

- NSLookup.

- Ping.

- Traceroute.

- Whois.

- NetStat.

These tools are often used together and are integrated with current operating systems (using a command prompt). Easier to use **graphical user interface (GUI)** versions of these tools are readily available on the Internet:

- Sam Spade   www.samspade.org

- Net Demon   www.netdemon.net

- Netscan Tools   www.netscantools.com

- Network Toolbox   www.ictcp.com/products/network-toolbox.html

For additional information on Internet address assignment and domain name registration, go to the following Web sites:

- Internet Corporation for Assigned Names and Numbers at www.icann.org

- Internet Assigned Numbers Authority at www.iana.org

- American Registry for Internet Numbers at www.arin.net

- Reseaux IP Europeans at www.ripe.net

- Asia Pacific Network Information Centre at www.apnic.net

- Latin American and Caribbean Internet Addresses Registry (LACNIC) at www.lacnic.net

STOP Suspects may monitor their own networks and detect the investigator's IP address and use of some of these tools. This in turn may alert suspects that their activities are being monitored. When it is important to conceal investigative activity, investigators should use a computer and Internet connection that cannot be traced to them or their agency.

NSLookup

Introduction

NSLookup is a utility that looks up, matches, and resolves domain names with IP addresses, and IP addresses with domain names.

Value of NSLookup

- To investigators:

  — Investigators use NSLookup to find the IP address from a domain name.

  — Identifying a domain name may provide information that ultimately leads to the identification of a target.

- To subjects:

  — Subjects use NSLookup to gain information about *domains* for target reconnaissance.

Identifying and obtaining NSLookup

- The NSLookup program is usually included with most operating systems and is available with numerous Internet investigative tools.

- The previously mentioned Web sites contain tools to accomplish this process.

- Some Web sites provide the ability to run an NSLookup (e.g., www.samspade.org).

Special investigatory and other considerations

- NSLookup is relatively easy to use; however, special training and knowledge may be necessary to decipher results.

STOP Suspects may monitor their own networks and detect the investigator's IP address and use of NSLookup. This in turn may alert suspects that their activities are being monitored. When it is important to conceal investigative activity, investigators should use a computer and Internet connection that cannot be traced to them or their agency.

Legal considerations

Generally there are no legal issues in using NSLookup.

Ping

Introduction

Ping is a utility that sends signals (packets) to another computer on a network (including the Internet) to see if it sends a return or an echo. If all the signals timeout, the computer may be disconnected from a network or unreachable for other reasons (e.g., behind a firewall). Ping only checks a computer connected to a network.

Value of Ping

- To investigators:

  — Investigators can use Ping to obtain an IP address for a domain or to determine whether another computer is currently connected to a network.

  — Investigators can use Ping for network troubleshooting.

- To subjects:

  — Subjects can use Ping the same way as law enforcement does.

  — Subjects can use Ping to identify possible targets for attack.

Identifying and obtaining Ping

- The Ping program is included with most operating systems.

- Ping is available with numerous Internet investigative tools.

- Some Web sites provide the ability to Ping another computer.

Special considerations

- Firewalls, network configuration, and IP address class may adversely affect Ping's reliability.

- Ping is easy to run but a negative response may be misleading. It takes knowledge of network architecture to interpret the results.

STOP Suspects may monitor their own networks and detect the investigator's IP address and use of Ping. This in turn may alert suspects that their activities are being monitored. When it is important to conceal investigative activity, investigators should use a computer and Internet connection that cannot be traced to them or their agency.

Legal considerations

Generally there are no legal issues in using Ping .

Traceroute

Introduction

Traceroute is a utility that shows the Internet route **network packets** take between the source computer and the destination de vice.

Value of Traceroute

- To investigators:

  — Law enforcement uses Traceroute to determine the net work location of a subject's computer, server, or device.

  — Law enforcement uses Traceroute to troubleshoot net works.

Note: Knowing the network location will not necessarily reveal the physical location of the computer, server, or device. Over time, the Traceroute may show different paths to the same device.

- To subjects:

  — Subjects use Traceroute to troubleshoot net works and find the network location of target computers, including those of the in vestigators.

Identifying and obtaining Traceroute

- Traceroute is included with most operating sy stems.

- Traceroute is available with numerous Internet investigative tools.

- Some Web sites provide the ability to run Traceroute.

Special investigatory and other considerations

- Firewalls, network configuration, and IP address may adversely affect Traceroute's reliability.

- The network location identified using Traceroute may not be accurate and should be verified by using other tools listed in this chapter.

- Traceroute is easy to run but takes training and knowledge to decipher the results.

STOP Suspects may monitor their own networks and detect the investigator's IP address and use of Traceroute. This in turn may alert suspects that their activities are being monitored. When it is important to conceal investigative activity, investigators should use a computer and Internet connection that cannot be traced to them or their agency.

Legal considerations

Generally there are no legal issues in using Traceroute.

Whois

Introduction

Whois is a utility that provides the recorded registration information for a domain name or IP address. Whois determines this information by searching one of several Internet registry databases. The information contained in these databases is provided by the registrant at the time of registration and may be changed by the registrant at any time. Therefore, this information may not be accurate.

Value of Whois

- To investigators:

  - Investigators use Whois to obtain domain name or IP address registration information.

  - Investigators may use Whois to identify the name servers that could be associated with the most recent ISP or Web host for that domain.

  - Whois can be used to identify people or entities to whom or to which legal processes can be served.

- To subjects:

  - Subjects use Whois to identify the responsible party or contact person for a domain.

  - Subjects can use Whois to obtain information about possible targets of their activity.

Identifying and obtaining Whois

- Whois is included with most operating systems.

- Whois is available with numerous Internet investigative tools.

- Some Web sites provide the ability to run Whois.

Special investigatory and other considerations

STOP The party named in the Whois entry may be the target of the investigation. Be aware that contact with the entities named in the Whois response may alert the subjects of the investigation.

- Different Whois servers *(registrars)* may contain different information so law enforcement may need to perform multiple Whois requests on multiple servers.

- Whois is easy to run but takes training to decipher the results.

- Information supplied by the registrant may not be accurate and may need to be independently verified.

- Some domains are registered to holding companies that act as an agent for the actual user. Blocks of IP addresses can be leased out to smaller providers. Accordingly, the entity to which the domain is registered may be different than the entity using the domain.

- The entity using the domain name may have hijacked it from the lawful owner or registrant.

STOP Suspects may monitor their own networks and detect the investigator's IP address and use of Whois. This in turn may alert suspects that their activities are being monitored. When it is important to conceal investigative activity, investigators should use a computer and Internet connection that cannot be traced to them or their agency.

Legal considerations

Generally there are no legal issues in using Whois.

Scenarios

1. Investigators receive information regarding terrorist threats made to a school via e-mail. They obtain the *header* of the e-mail and use Internet tools to help identify the sender of the threat. (For more information, *see Investigations Involving the Internet and Computer Networks)* (www.ojp.usdoj.gov/nij/pubs-sub/210798.htm)).

2. An investigator uses Whois to obtain the contact information for the Internet service provider of the IP address in an investigation. The investigator serves a subpoena on the entity listed, not realizing that the registrant is actually the subject of the investigation. This alerts the subject, who shuts down his illegal operation.

Netstat

Introduction

Netstat (network status) is a utility that displays the services (e.g., FTP, Telnet), IP connections, and **ports** that are currently open on the computer running the command. For example, Netstat may show a computer's link to a subject's computer during an online file transfer or session.

Value of Netstat

■ To investigators:

— Netstat allows an investigator to determine what network connections are open on a computer. This may help the investigator determine whether the computer has a **back door** or **Trojan**.

— Investigators can identify the IP address of a computer with which the investigator is communicating or connected.

— With proper training, an investigator can use Netstat on a computer to determine live connections. This may identify leads that help determine what the subject was using the network for. Seek expert assistance if not fully experienced with the utility as use will change the data on the computer.

STOP Running Netstat on a subject's computer will change the state of the data on that computer. While changing the data on a subject's computer is generally discouraged, a balance between crucial evidence gained and alterations made to the system must be considered. Seek expert assistance to run this utility. Also, based on the content of an existing warrant or consent, be aware that additional legal authority may be required to retrieve this data.

■ To subjects:

— Subjects can use Netstat to determine the IP address and port of connection of their computer.

Identifying and obtaining Netstat

■ Netstat is included with most operating systems.

■ Netstat is available with numerous Internet investigative tools.

Special investigatory and other considerations

STOP Initiating a direct connection (for the purpose of running Netstat) may alert suspects of investigative activity. When it is important to conceal investigative activity, investigators should use a computer and Internet connection that cannot be traced to them or their agency.

Legal considerations

Generally there are no legal issues in using Netstat.

Scenarios

1. During an undercover child pornography investigation, a suspect establishes a direct connection to the undercover officer to transmit a photograph. During that session, the investigator uses Netstat to determine the IP of the suspect's machine.

2. During the execution of a search warrant, a trained network investigator runs Netstat on a subject's computer to determine connections between that computer and a compromised government system to which the subject did not have authorized access.

Keystroke monitoring

Hardware keystroke capturing device

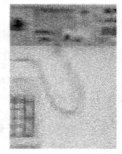

Before installation of logger

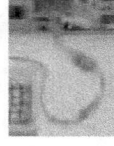

After installation of logger

Introduction

Keystroke monitoring tools allow for the monitoring and recording of keyboard activity on a computer. This can be accomplished through the use of either hardware or software. In contrast, those devices that capture bidirectional network traffic are known as sniffers, which are discussed later in this guide.

Value of keystroke monitoring

■ To investigators:

— Keystroke monitoring is useful for password retrieval and profiling activity (what a user is doing) in addition to answering the following questions:

■ Where are they going (what Web sites)?

■ With whom are they communicating?

■ What type of data are they creating?

■ Are they accessing or transmitting sensitive or proprietary information or contraband?

    — Investigators may use keystroke monitoring to log their own activity during under-cover operations.

■ To subjects:

    — Keystroke monitoring can be used in the same manner as any other surveillance tool to covertly gather the following:

      ■ Information for identity theft on public machines.

      ■ User names and passwords.

      ■ Economic information from corporate computers.

      ■ Usage of the computer by a domestic partner.

Identifying and obtaining keystroke monitoring

■ Hardware and software keystroke loggers are available from retail and custom equipment resources. For specific information regarding obtaining keystroke loggers, check with the following:

    — Surveillance equipment providers for details about acquisition, cost, and use. Vendors might provide a "Law Enforcement Only" version with special features or special pricing.

    — Other agencies or corporate security departments for available hardware loan equipment.

    — Other agencies that may be willing to provide technical or material assistance.

    — **_Shareware_** Web sites for keystroke software.

■ Identifying keystroke capturing hardware:

    — Hardware devices come in a variety of forms. Look for the following:

      ■ Special keyboards that log keystrokes.

      ■ Devices connected between the keyboard and the PC.

      ■ Devices located inside the PC case, making them less visble.

      ■ Surveillance cameras ("shoulder surfing") that record the activity of the user at the keyboard.

■ Identifying keystroke capturing software:

    — Software can be identified through forensic examination.

Special investigatory and other considerations

- Keystroke monitoring can be used in situations such as the following:

  — The user is accessing encrypted files, password-protected Web sites, or password-protected systems (local or remote) to capture the passphrase.

  — The user is creating threatening e-mails or sharing trade secrets to capture the content of the e-mail without accessing the file itself.

  — A computer is in a common area being used for questionable activity. Keystroke monitoring can be used in combination with a video camera to establish not only what is being done, but who is performing the activity.

- General notes on use:

  — Be sure to record the system time of the computer on which the keystroke monitor is installed in order to establish a known time for the activity.

  — Be sure to record the version of the operating system on the subject's machine.

- Other considerations for use:

  — Determine the capabilities of the keystroke monitoring tool prior to use.

  — Some keystroke monitoring programs also provide for the capability of a full screen capture of all activity that appears on the computer display, in real time.

    ▪ The advantage of this type of monitoring is that it captures typed input, mouse clicks, and desktop navigation.

    ▪ The disadvantage is the amount of data storage that is required to preserve the capture.

  — Some keystroke monitoring programs can e-mail activity logs directly to a designated individual on a scheduled basis (e.g., hourly, daily, weekly), but this outbound e-mail notification may be detectable by the subject of the investigation.

  — Some keystroke monitoring programs can be configured to capture and log only selected information to comply with *minimization* requirements.

  — When using shareware keystroke monitoring software, remember:

    ▪ It may not have the full functionality of a commercial product.

    ▪ It may have minimal technical support available.

  — The keystroke monitoring tool should be tested on a similar system to identify potential problems prior to employing it during an investigation.

  — If the keystroke monitoring hardware or software requires physical installation, consult a qualified technician.

— Follow agency or department guidelines on covert operations, and consult with legal counsel before employing keystroke monitoring tools.

■ Limitations:

— Physical access to the target computer or the results file may be limited.

— Capacity of the keystroke monitoring device or target computer to store results over a given period of time may be limited.

— Consider using software that allows remote access to the tool and results. Security software or hardware used by the subject may prevent remote access.

— The subject may be alerted to the presence of keystroke monitors for the following reasons:

    ▪ Hardware devices may be visble to the subject.

    ▪ Software keystroke monitoring programs may trigger the subject's virus detection software, appear in the taskbar or process listings, or cause anomalous behavior if they are not compatible with other applications.

    ▪ Spyware detection programs may detect software keystroke monitoring programs, disable them, and alert the subject.

Legal considerations

It is not illegal to purchase or possess keystroke monitoring hardware or software. However, there are many legal considerations in installing and using these tools.

■ Installation:

— Investigators must have lawful access to the computer on which the tool or software is installed. Often those using computers connected to a network give their consent through banners or written consent. If there is no consent, investigators will need a search warrant or other legal process to install the software or tool.

— If shoulder surfing is used to videotape activity on a computer in an area where a person has a reasonable expectation of privacy, investigators will be required to obtain a search warrant or other legal process to install the video camera.

■ Use:

— The real-time interception of a person's communications requires either the user's consent or a Title III or State wiretap order. Generally, unless the subject has given consent to keystroke monitoring, a wiretap order is required.

— Retrieving the data and uninstalling software that collected the keystroke monitoring data require lawful access to the subject's computer.

— Wiretap orders should address all the activities that the investigator needs to conduct, including covert entry and reentry to install the device, monitoring the device, retrieving the data, retrieving and maintaining any device, and uninstalling any software.

— It is a violation of Title III and State wiretap statutes for an individual—whether a law enforcement officer or a private person—to intercept in real time the private communications of another without a wiretap order or consent. Violators may be subject to criminal and civil liability.

— Consent can be obtained through network or entity banners or written consent. A banner that permits keystroke monitoring, however, might not permit physical access to the computer to be monitored.

— It can be illegal to use information collected in violation of Title III or State wiretap statutes. Any information so obtained may be unusable or suppressed. Should investigators be offered the results of keystroke monitoring collected by another, they should consult legal counsel before examining the data.

— Some jurisdictions may require consent from all parties involved in the communication or a wiretap order. Consult with legal counsel to determine the correct course of action.

STOP Consult legal counsel before engaging in keystroke monitoring or advising others, such as parents, to use such software.

Scenarios

1. During an investigation of a suspect using encryption software, the investigator installs a keystroke logger on a computer to which the investigator has physical and legal access to capture the passphrases used by the suspect prior to seizing his computer.

2. In a public Internet access terminal, a user installs a keystroke capture device. The information the user obtains from other users at that terminal enables him to commit identity theft and other financial crimes.

Mass media copiers and duplicators

Mass media duplicator

CD and DVD duplicator

Introduction

Mass media copiers and duplicators (including DVD and CD burners, floppy duplicators, and hard drive duplicators) copy media in bulk. The devices may retain data from the duplicated media. They may also maintain records pertaining to recent actions performed by a device.

Value of mass media copiers and duplicators

- To investigators:

  — Mass media duplicators may have historical information that can provide proof of duplication.

  — Mass media duplicators can assist with preparing discovery or large amounts of evidence.

- To subjects:

  — Possession of mass media duplicators may be evidence of software piracy, copyright infringement, or duplication of contraband material.

Identifying and obtaining mass media copiers and duplicators

Mass media copiers and duplicators are commercially available.

Special investigatory and other considerations

Owners of copyrighted material or their represent atives may be willing to assist investigators if their materials are the subject of unlawful duplication (e.g., Motion Picture Association of America (MPAA) (www.mpaa.org), Recording Industry Association of America (RIAA) (www.riaa.com), and Business Software Alliance (BSA) (www.bsa.org)).

Legal considerations

- Seizing or searching these devices implicates the Fourth Amendment.

- When the presence of these devices is suspected, search warrants should include the ability to search for the original and any copies of the source media.

- Consult with prosecutors concerning violations of F ederal and State criminal law(s) (e.g., intellectual property, theft, trademark infringement).

- Consult the **Digital Millennium Copyright Act (DMCA)** for guidance in cases of copyright infringement.

See Chapter 3, Legal Issues, for more information.

Pagers

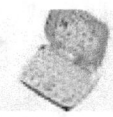 

Introduction

Some pagers receive only numeric messages, but more advanced pagers can send and receive alphanumeric messages. For example, **BlackBerry**® devices allow sending and receiving e-mail, among other capabilities. In addition to the inf ormation on the device itself, numbers or text may be maintained by the service provider.

Value of pagers

- To investigators:

  — Searching pagers may reveal the telephone numbers of a subject's accomplices and when the subject communicated with them.

  — Searching pagers can reveal coded messages accomplices might send.

- To subjects:

  — Subjects use pagers to send or receive messages that may contain coded information.

  — Subjects can use pagers to store information.

Identifying and obtaining pagers

- These items are commercially available.

- Pagers can be self-contained devices or built into PDAs or cell phones.

Special investigatory and other considerations

- Information stored on a pager is volatile.

  — Pagers have finite memory and should be searched as soon as legally permissible to retrieve existing data. This will help prevent incoming messages from overwriting stored data.

  — Some pagers lose their data when power is interrupted; therefore, investigators should be prepared to replace the existing power source.

  — There are techniques to prevent a pager from receiving information without powering it off, such as putting the pager in a clean paint can or other metal container (see *Best Practices for Seizing Electronic Evidence, Version 2* (www.fletc.gov/legal/downloads/bestpractices.pdf), for more information).

  — Investigators should balance the usefulness of monitoring incoming messages with the need to keep stored data on the pager.

Legal considerations

- Seizing or searching pagers implicates the Fourth Amendment.

- Real-time interception of pager information (e.g., use of ***cloned pagers***) implicates wiretap statutes.

- To obtain records of inbound pages or text messages being retained by service providers, consult chapter 3 for information on ECPA.

See Chapter 3, Legal Issues, for more information.

Pens and traps

Introduction

Pen registers (pens) record the numbers as they are dialed from a specific phone number (outbound calls). A trap and trace (traps) records the telephone numbers as they are received by a specific phone number (inbound calls). These processes also are used to identify e-mail and IP addresses of senders and recipients in real time. Pens and traps are not intended to capture the content of the communications, but only the telephone number, IP, or e-mail address. Pens and traps may also provide location information for wireless telephones.

Value of pens and traps

- To investigators:

  — Investigators can use pen registers and trap and trace to do the following:

    - Learn the telephone numbers a subject is calling or those numbers from which the subject is receiving calls.

    - Locate fugitives and others.

    - Trace assets by identifying relevant banking institutions.

    - Determine phone numbers of ISPs dialed.

    - Determine online activity (e.g., dates and times of connections), which would also confirm that there is a computer at the location to be searched.

    - Determine when, from where, and in what order conspirators are communicating.

    - Determine the e-mail and IP addresses of a subject's correspondents.

    - Determine the location of a wireless telephone.

- To subjects:

  — Traps and traces are legal processes available only to law enforcement.

  — Subjects can obtain similar information as that provided by pens and traps by using a "call dialed," "call received," or caller ID function on their phones.

Identifying and obtaining pens and traps

- Pens and traps are usually accomplished by using existing software and hardware at the Internet service or telecommunications provider.

- Those communications service providers that do not have the capability to provide the information may require investigators or telephone technicians to install a ***dialed number recorder (DNR)*** to capture outgoing calls.

- The above would also apply when investigators elect not to use the services of the telecommunications provider to provide pen and trap information (e.g., when telecommunications employees are the target of the investigation).

Special investigatory and other considerations

- When investigators want pen and trap information for past calls, they should obtain toll records or detailed billing information from the service provider. (See the section on ECPA in Chapter 3, Legal Issues, for more information.)

- Some of these devices have alternative uses (e.g., a DNR can be used to translate stored tone or pulse data in a speed dial memory).

Legal considerations

- Obtaining a pen or trap requires a court order or consent of the subscriber.

- The **Federal Pen and Trap Statute** does not apply to obtaining information from caller ID boxes, speed dialers, cell phones, and like devices or features because the information is recovered after the call or electronic communication has been made. However, the Fourth Amendment is implicated in seizing and searching these devices.

Scenario

In a drug investigation, a trap and trace order is obtained for several suspected dealers. The data obtained include hundreds of incoming telephone calls. By using a computer program to show links among the numbers, the investigator is able to identify co-conspirators and eventually move up in the supply chain.

Personal digital assistants

Introduction

Personal digital assistants (PDAs) are handheld computers designed with similar capabilities as those available on a standard computer such as a personal information management functions (e.g., calendar, contacts, to-do list, e-mail), a word processor, and spreadsheet and database utilities. PDAs may also include the following capabilities:

- Camera (still or video).

- GPS.

- E-mail.

- Voice mail.

- Text messaging.

- Infrared transmission.

- Wireless network capability *(802.11)*.

- Bluetooth®.

- Web browsing capability.

- Data storage (digital card).

- Voice recording.

- Telephony (VoIP) and cellular communications.

- PDA software is available online to accomplish any task.

Value of PDAs

- To investigators:

  — Investigators can use PDAs for the following:

    - Managing cases.

    - Storing important reference material such as addresses or PDF files.

    - Sending and receiving e-mail with attachments that may contain evidence.

    - Brief note taking.

    - Storing templates of commonly used documents or forms (go-bys) for immediate access in the field.

    - Determining the precise location of the device (when GPS enabled).

  — Forensic analysis of a subject's PDA may reveal information of investigative value such as the following:

    - Phone or contact lists.

    - E-mails and text messages.

    - Calendars and schedules.

- Documents and financial records.

- Notes and digital voice or video recordings.

- Information that may be used to impeach the subject's later testimony.

- Other information related to knowledge, motive, intent, and association with victim or accomplices.

■ To subjects:

— The value of a PDA is limited only by a subject's creativity and the technical capability of the particular device.

Identifying and obtaining PDAs

■ PDAs are generally handheld and may be stored or carried almost anywhere.

■ PDAs are commonly **synchronized** with one or more personal computers. Therefore, if an investigator finds a PDA, the investigator should consider the probability that there is an affiliated computer. Similarly, if the investigator discovers a computer with a cradle or other synchronizing device attached, the investigator should consider taking steps to locate the corresponding device.

Special investigatory and other considerations

■ **STOP** Critical power-related issues with PDAs:

— Powering up a PDA will alter data. If seizing a PDA found in the off position, leave it off. If seizing a PDA that is on, photograph and document the data on the screen and then consult a person knowledgeable in powering down or examining PDAs. For more information, see the USSS *Best Practices for Seizing Electronic Evidence, Version 2* (www.fletc.gov/legal/downloads/bestpractices.pdf) or *Guidelines on PDA Forensics: Recommendations of the National Institute of Standards and Technology SP–800–72 and PDA Forensic Tools: An Overview and Analysis NISTIR 7100* (http://csrc.nist.gov/publications/nistir/nistir-7100-PDAForensics.pdf).

— PDAs that lose power can lose data. Be sure to also seize all PDA accessories including cradles, power cords, etc. Ensure that the PDA has a continuous source of power while in long-term storage.

■ Data contained on a PDA may also be found on computers. Investigators should obtain legal authority to search computers associated with any PDA examined.

Legal considerations

■ The search and seizure of a PDA implicates the Fourth Amendment.

■ The authority to seize a PDA may not be sufficient to search it.

- Legal process to seize and search a PDA should also request authority to seize and search chargers, cradles, and associated computers.

- Legal process should also request the authority to look for passwords to decrypt or access the data on the PDA.

- When a PDA is used as a communication device or mobile phone, consult the section on cell phones, legal considerations, in this chapter.

- Consult Chapter 3, Legal Issues, for additional information.

Scenario

Common mistakes:

A police officer seizes a PDA in an investigation.

- He places it in the evidence room without a power source and the PDA loses battery power, resulting in the loss of all evidence contained in the device.

- The PDA is on, but the officer allows the device to go into suspend mode. Because bringing it out requires a password, the officer can no longer access the data.

- The PDA is off and the officer turns it on. Doing this modifies the data.

Following the above suggestions and references can help avoid these potentially serious mistakes.

Removable storage media and players

Portable media players   Portable media player/voice recorder

USB watch   MP3 player/watch with USB cable

USB pen

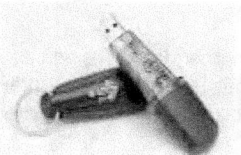

USB flash drive on keychain

Swiss army knife USB

Secure digital (SD) card

Firewire drive

"HotDrive" USB 2 0/FireWire (IEEE 1394) 2.5" Combo Enclosure

Zip® drive

External hard drive

Introduction

Removable storage media comes in numerous forms and sizes capable of storing large amounts of information. In order to interface with a computer they may require a separate media reader. Some storage media may not be readily recognizable as computer accessories.

Value of removable storage media

- To investigators:

  — These devices may contain evidence of criminal activity.

  — Investigators may use these devices to store and exchange work product.

  — Investigators may use these devices to provide discovery.

- To subjects:

  — Subjects may use these devices to store, hide, and exchange information.

  — Because of the portability of these devices, they can be easily concealed.

Identifying and obtaining removable storage media

- These devices can be located virtually anywhere (e.g., **flash media** containing contraband or other evidence stored in a digital sewing machine).

- Many of these devices require special cables, cradles, power supplies, or other equipment to connect the media to an output device. The presence of these items indicates that the subject is using removable storage media.

- A wide variety of removable storage media is available. Note that the devices can be extremely small. Examples:

  — CDs, DVDs, and other optical media.

  — **MP3 players** (can store more than music).

  — Zip® disks.

  — Floppy disks.

  — **FireWire** devices.

  — **Microdrives.**

  — **Personal Computer Memory Card Interface Association (PCMCIA)** devices.

  — **Universal Serial Bus (USB) drives or devices** (see below).

  — Flash media.

- ThumbDrives® are a form of flash media that are commonly connected to computers through USB ports. These devices can be small and integrated into pens, watches, jewelry, etc.

- Other forms of flash media include CompactFlash, Memory Sticks, Secure Digital Cards (SDC), SmartMedia Cards, Reduced Size Multi-Media Cards (RS–MMC), Multi-Media Cards (MMC), MiniSD Card, and xD Picture Cards. These media are often used in handheld devices and may be connected to a computer through USB or FireWire adaptors and readers designed to handle multiple formats.

- Hard drives are normally found inside a computer. They can also be used as a portable device externally and can be connected to a computer via FireWire, USB, or through a wireless connection. Wireless hard drives can be hidden (e.g., in a false ceiling) and remotely accessed by multiple computers.

Special investigatory and other considerations

- Because of the portability of these devices, they can be easily concealed.

- If magnetic tapes are recovered or acquired, ensure that appropriate equipment is available for their examination or restoration. Alternatively, the information can be restored to other types of media that can be more easily analyzed. The recovery of tapes is likely to occur when businesses or corporations are involved.

STOP Digital information in these devices can be easily altered. See the section on volatility of digital evidence in chapter 1 for more information.

Legal considerations

- Seizing or searching removable storage media usually implicates the Fourth Amendment.

- The authority to seize removable storage media does not necessarily include the authority to search it.

See Chapter 3, Legal Issues, for more information.

Scenario

During booking of a subject suspected of child exploitation, the subject drops a thumbnail-sized storage card. The booking officer sees the object fall, notices a change of expression on the subject's face, and retrieves the card. Examination of the card reveals evidence implicating the subject in the crime.

Sniffers

Introduction

The term "sniffer" refers to a device or software that captures communication information directly from a network and can be the computer network equivalent of a wiretap, depending on the level of detail captured. The information collected includes network packet information, which provides the source and destination of communications. A sniffer can also capture full communication content.

Sniffers are often employed legitimately by communication providers (e.g., universities, government agencies, and ISPs) and corporate information technology (IT) departments in an effort to protect and monitor their computer networks. Monitoring the information captured by a sniffer can alert security professionals to an illegal network intrusion or misuse of network resources by employees.

Value of sniffers

- To investigators:

    — Information gathered by a network sniffer may provide an investigator with the source IP address of a communication.

    — Full content capture can provide a complete record of the following:

        - Data transferred (including the data itself).

        - Incriminating or evidentiary communications (electronic mail, etc.).

        - The existence and possible identification of accomplices.

        - The modus operandi of the subject.

- To subjects:

    — Sniffers are installed by subjects in order to gather information. Sniffers are commonly used to do the following:

        - Identify users.

        - Gather passwords.

        - Identify computers on a network.

        - Steal data.

        - Monitor communication (illegal wiretap).

Identifying and obtaining sniffers

- A sniffer has no single physical identifying feature and can be difficult to detect.

- A sniffer can be a dedicated computer running specialized software and connected to a network at a data "bottleneck." All incoming and outgoing traffic can be monitored. When used internally by an agency or corporate security department to monitor its own network, a sniffer may be included as part of an ***intrusion detection system (IDS).*** There are commercial IDS packages available online and from security software vendors.

- A sniffer can be a small covert program installed on a single desktop computer that collects all network traffic visible to that computer. These programs are very popular with hackers and are easily hidden. They are available online.

Special investigatory and other considerations

- Corporations and agencies often retain IDS archives or logs. These can be obtained for investigative purposes.

- Sniffers can generate huge amounts of data, depending on the size and activity of a network (number of computers, amount of traffic). Investigators need to be aware of the potential volume of data when requesting IDS logs. Such requests should be as specific in scope as possible.

- If the subject is using encrypted communications, the data captured by the sniffer (though not the header information) will be similarly encrypted.

- Request copies of banners and user agreements (see Legal Considerations section below for more information).

Legal considerations

- Even in those jurisdictions where it is legal to possess sniffer tools, some uses may implicate the Fourth Amendment, wiretap laws, and ECPA.

  — The use of sniffer data is legally sensitive and may implicate wiretap statutes. Although data can be obtained voluntarily or through legal process in a number of ways, it is always advisable to consult legal counsel before proceeding.

Scenario

1. An investigator is called to a local company that has had several computer systems compromised by an intruder. Analysis of one of the affected computers reveals sniffer log files maintained and accessed periodically by the intruder. The intruder has been gathering network traffic inside the company. The sniffer logs contain the network names of other computers in the company, user names, and passwords. Using this information, the investigator is able to identify other victim computers and compromised user accounts at the company for further analysis and evidence.

2. A State agency suspects an employee of transmitting sensitive data from his computer at work to his home Internet account. Because that particular user has access to a number of computer systems, the investigators decide to install a sniffer at the agency "firewall." Network traffic captured by the sniffer gives the investigators the

time, date, originating and destination IP addresses, and the content of the emplo yee's transmission, including the suspect dat a. Through the use of witnesses and sur veillance cameras, investigators are able to place the suspect at the k eyboard of the originating computer at the time of the illicit transmission.

Steganography

Introduction

Steganography is the process of concealing a file within the dat a of a carrier file. Taken from the Greek, the word literally means "concealed writing." Steganalysis is the process of locating and subsequently obt aining the concealed dat a from an image. Although the most common types of files used to cont ain concealed dat a are image files, several programs are available that will conceal dat a within other **file types** as well. Data hidden in a carrier file may also be encr ypted for additional securit y.

Value of steganography

- To investigators:

  — Investigators may mark images that are transmit ted during online investigations, permitting the investigator to identify positiv ely and conclusively image files during court testimony that were transmitted to suspects during the in vestigation.

  — Investigators may conceal and encr ypt data to make it available for transmission through unsecured channels. Review agency policies on appro ved use of this technique.

- To subjects:

  — Subjects use steganograph y to hinder or prevent the discovery of evidence by investigators.

  — Subjects may use steganography to hide and transmit inf ormation through Web pages.

Obtaining and identifying steganography tools

- Various steganography programs are available as freeware through the Internet.

- Some steganography tools are very small programs that require no inst allation. Related files (if necessary) are designed to be placed in the director y from which the program is executed. As a result, these programs could be maint ained and run from removable media.

Special investigatory and other considerations

- Encryption implemented within steganography programs may be too robust to defeat.

- The carrier file and the source file containing the original data existed as separate data files at one time. Locating these data files may be the only means of defeating the process.

- Locating removable media may be paramount in cases where steganography is suspected.

Legal considerations

- It is legal for the public to possess and use steganography software. In some circumstances, however, possession or use of steganography software may indicate criminal activity.

- There are no legal restrictions on investigators using steganography analysis tools provided the data or media being examined is lawfully acquired.

Vehicle black boxes and navigation systems

Introduction

Many vehicles (e.g., cars, planes, trains, boats, farm equipment) produced today contain black boxes or navigation systems that are capable of capturing data regarding the vehicle's operation, status, and location. These devices can also be after-market addons.

Value of vehicle black boxes and navigation systems

- To investigators:

  — Just like the black box on an airplane, black boxes installed in other vehicles will capture potentially valuable information such as the operational history of a vehicle.

  — Certain devices, such as OnStar®, LoJack®, or built-in cellular phones can assist in identifying the physical location of the vehicle that contains them. (See section on GPS Devices.)

  — Automated toll collection devices, such as EZPass℠, can provide information as to previously traveled routes.

  — Vehicle navigation systems may store route history and previously programmed or saved GPS waypoints.

  — Certain devices such as OnStar® allow two-way communication with or the monitoring of communications within the vehicle.

— Rental car companies may use navigation systems to monitor the location and operation of their cars. This information may be maintained by the rental company and made available to investigators.

— The information available from these devices can be used for the following:

■ Accident reconstruction.

■ To pinpoint the physical location of a vehicle.

■ To determine speed.

■ To monitor conversations in a vehicle.

■ To subjects:

— Subjects can use vehicular navigation systems to plan routes; track shipments; and pinpoint locations, people, or objects.

Note: Black boxes are not normally accessed by the vehicle operator. Black boxes are placed on vehicles by manufacturers for diagnostic purposes.

Identifying and obtaining vehicle black boxes and navigation systems

■ Navigation systems are either installed in the vehicle prior to purchase or can be obtained after market.

■ Black boxes are typically installed by the manufacturer of the vehicle.

Special investigatory and other considerations

■ Information may be available on the device itself or from a third-party service provider.

■ More than one of these devices may be in any given vehicle.

Legal considerations

■ Seizing or searching vehicle black boxes and navigation systems may implicate Fourth Amendment concerns.

■ Obtaining information from third-party service providers may raise ECPA or State-specific issues pertaining to the recovery of electronic data.

■ With a wiretap order, law enforcement may intercept the content of mobile communication devices.

Refer to Chapter 3, Legal Issues, for additional information.

Scenario

A woman stopped at a red light with a child in the back seat. The car was carjacked with the child still in the car. As the woman was pulled from the car by the carjacker, she pressed the OnStar® button, activating the service. Officers were able to listen to conversations in the vehicle as well as track the location of the vehicle until the carjacker was apprehended.

Video and digital image analysis tools

Introduction

These tools aid the examiner in the acquisition, processing, and output of images to assist in the examination of the video and digital images. The use of the word "image" in this section should not be confused with the process of imaging or copying a hard drive. This section addresses the following:

- Digital still images (a photograph in digital form).

- Digital video images.

- Conventional photographs and analog videos and movies that have been converted to a digital format.

Value of digital tools

- To investigators. By using these tools the examiner may do the following:

  — Enhance details of the image.

  — Authenticate the image to do the following:

    ▪ Determine the source or origin.

    ▪ Determine whether the image has been altered.

  — Duplicate imagery.

  — Convert images to other formats.

  — Conduct forensic examinations that may reveal features not otherwise obvious. For example, these techniques may reveal traces of ***indented*** or obliterated handwriting.

  — Compare known and questioned images to identify or eliminate items depicted as coming from the same source. For example, an examination can compare facial features and clothing from surveillance cameras to known images of a subject and the subject's clothing.

  — Determine height, length, and other dimensional information from an image (photogrammetry).

— Use age progression or regression techniques to simulate younger or older appearances of a subject.

■ To subjects:

— Most of the tools considered here are publicly available. Subjects may use these tools to alter original images. For example, a subject may modify a picture to support an alibi or insert contraband images into a legitimate video file.

— These tools can also be used to produce false identification or to counterfeit securities, currency, and documents.

Identifying and obtaining digital tools

■ Identification of the tools needed depends on the types of examinations being conducted. Software, hardware, and photographic and video equipment used in the examinations are publicly available.

■ Forensic digital imaging and video applications and examinations are very complex, so care should be given when determining what equipment and software to acquire.

■ Be cautious of integrated ("turnkey") systems, as they may not provide the required capabilities and equipment for your agency.

■ Costs vary greatly. Depending on need, some examinations can be accomplished using inexpensive off-the-shelf hardware and software. For example, a basic computer and projector may be adequate in some cases.

Special investigatory and other considerations

■ The degree of training needed to use these tools varies greatly. Advanced skills may be needed to analyze and interpret data.

■ Examiners must be careful to analyze only copies and not original files.

Legal considerations

■ Software tools should have appropriate licensing agreements.

■ There are generally no other legal considerations, provided that the file being examined has been lawfully acquired.

Voice recorder (digital)

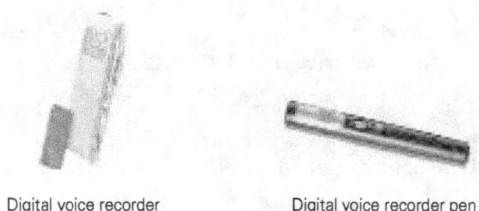

Digital voice recorder   Digital voice recorder pen

Introduction

Digital voice recorders record sound. These small devices can contain many hours of voice. Some of the devices may also write to mini-CDs or other removable media.

Value of digital voice recorders

- To investigators:

  — Investigators can record information (e.g., notes and interviews) in the field.

  — Investigators can make surreptitious audio recordings (ensure compliance with wire-tap laws).

  — Digital voice recorders and their removable media can contain evidence of crime such as notes, confessions, diaries, environmental sounds, and conversations.

- To subjects:

  — Subjects can use digital voice recorders to record notes and diaries that may relate to criminal activity.

  — These devices can be used to surreptitiously record conversations.

  — Some digital voice recorders are capable of holding data (e.g., photographs) other than sound recordings.

  — Devices can be used to alter a recording to create alternate versions of events.

Identifying and obtaining digital voice recorders

- Digital voice recorders can look like or be integrated into numerous devices such as pens, watches, cell phones, MP3 players, PDAs, and key chains. These devices are commercially available.

- Data can be stored on the device or transferred to a computer through wireless as well as wired connections such as a cradle device or USB.

- Some devices have removable media that can be read directly by a computer.

Special investigatory and other considerations

STOP Some digital voice recorders require constant power to retain memory. If power loss is a possibility, consider recording the digital voice recorder's output to preserve the data. (See Fourth Amendment section in Chapter 3, Legal Issues.)

- The file format of the information stored on digital voice recorders may be proprietary, requiring special equipment, software, or manufacturer guidance.

- Examine the device to determine whether investigators should also search for removable storage media.

- Removable media can hold any information capable of being digitized. Therefore, the information available from analysis of the removable media may not be something that was originally recorded on the voice recorder. For example, an image file could be found on the Memory Stick of a digital voice recorder.

Legal considerations

- Seizure of the digital voice recorder and information that has been transferred from it to a computer implicates the Fourth Amendment.

See Chapter 3, Legal Issues, for more information.

Chapter 3. Legal Issues for the Use of High Technology

Introduction

Criminal investigations that involve the use of technology or the collection of digital evidence are governed at the Federal and State levels by a number of constitutional and statutory provisions, court decisions, procedural rules, and industry-specific laws.

This chapter begins with a review of Fourth Amendment principles, focusing on seizing and searching computers and other electronic devices. The Fourth Amendment review is followed by statutes that, in some cases, provide more protection than the Fourth Amendment provides.

Investigators, examiners, and prosecutors should be familiar with these requirements because their breach may result in evidentiary challenge or civil suit. Other Federal provisions and State law are beyond the scope of this guide.

Constitutional issues

Searches for digital evidence, like searches for other forms of evidence, are subject to the constraints of Federal and State constitutional and statutory search and seizure laws. Traditional Fourth Amendment principles apply to digital evidence.

Application of the Fourth Amendment

The Fourth Amendment protects individuals from unreasonable searches and seizures. The two primary requirements for Fourth Amendment protections to be invoked are the following:

- Is government action involved?

- Does the person affected have a reasonable expectation of privacy in the place or thing to be searched?

Government action. Government action is implicated when a government employee or agent conducts a search. Generally speaking, the Fourth Amendment's limitations do not apply to searches by private parties unless those searches are conducted at the direction or request of the government. Private parties who independently acquire evidence of a crime may turn it over to law enforcement, and the evidence may be used to further the investigation. In addition, law enforcement agents may replicate the private search but not exceed the scope of the private search without a warrant or exception to the warrant requirement.

For example, if a technician discovers contraband files on a computer being repaired in a shop and turns them over to law enforcement, the Fourth Amendment is not implicated. In such a case, law enforcement may examine only data that the technician observed. To proceed further, legal process would be required.

Reasonable expectation of privacy. The Fourth Amendment applies when a person has an expectation of privacy in the thing searched, and then only if it is an expectation that society is prepared to recognize as reasonable.

Satisfying Fourth Amendment requirements. If the Fourth Amendment is implicated in the search at issue, law enforcement must obtain a search warrant unless an exception to the warrant requirement applies.

Searches and seizures pursuant to warrants

If the Fourth Amendment is implicated in the search, law enforcement officers should obtain a warrant to search computers and electronic devices.

There is always a strong preference for obtaining warrants to search computers and electronic devices. Sometimes the standard Fourth Amendment exceptions used by officers in their everyday work—search incident to arrest, plain view, and exigent circumstances—will justify only the warrantless seizure of the computer or device; the actual search for the information contained on the device usually requires a warrant.

For example, a suspect in custody on a detention order was seen deleting possibly incriminating information from his PDA and a nearby detective seized the device without a warrant. Nevertheless, the exigency ended with the seizure, so the detective needed to obtain a warrant to examine the PDA. (See *U.S.* v. *David,* 756 F. Supp. 1385 (D. Nev., 1991)).

Because consent may be limited in scope and is revocable, warrants may be advisable even when consent has been obtained.

Generally, the same warrant rules apply when preparing and executing a warrant for digital evidence as for other investigations. Investigators should also consider the following when preparing and executing search warrants:

Describing property

Hardware. When the evidence sought is a known computer or device (the hardware is an instrumentality or the fruit of the crime or contains contraband), then the warrant should particularly descr be the computer as the t arget of the search and the location of the evidence sought.

Data. If the evidence sought is information that could be stored on digit al media, the warrant should particularly describe that information. The warrant should request the authority to search for and seize the information in whatever form it may be stored (e.g., paper or digital media).

STOP Avoid drafting warrants that would unnecessarily restrict the scope of the searc h. Ensure the warrant includes authority to look for ownership and control over any informa- tion of evidentiary value discovered on digit al media.

Note: For sample language, consult *Searching and Seizing Computers and Obtaining Electronic Evidence in Criminal Investigations* (www.cybercrime.gov/s&smanual 2002.htm).

Seized but unexamined media

In circumstances in which the computer or device has already been seized, the "place to be searched" described in the warrant may be the current location of the computer, and the devices being searched should be specifically identified.

Scenarios

1. A computer repair technician reports the presence of child pornography on a computer being serviced. The police seize the computer based on exigent circumstances. In drafting the warrant, the police describe the place to be searched as the computer's brand and model, located in the police propert y room at the property room address.

2. During the investigation of a murder, numerous items from the residence of the victim are seized, including a computer and PDA. These items are stored in the property room while normal investigatory processes are pursued. During the investigation, it is determined that information on the computer may contain evidence or leads. Therefore, the police obtain a warrant in which the police describe the place to be searched as the computer's brand and model, located in the police propert y room at the property room address.

3. During the investigation of a spree killing, a handwritten note was found at the scene of one of the victims st ating that the victim would no longer be able to vie w "that stuff" on the Internet any longer. Based on this evidence, a search warrant was served on the victim's computer, which was seized from the homicide victim's residence. Days later, upon the arrest of a suspect, a search of the suspect's residence resulted in the seizure of his computer. Based on the handwritten note, the search warrant for that computer was obtained.

Conducting the search

The search of an electronic storage device usually requires significant technical knowledge and should be conducted by appropriate personnel. Such personnel should be supplied with a copy of the search warrant and affidavit to ensure that the search is within the scope of the warrant.

In the course of conducting a search, an investigator may discover passwords and keys that could facilitate access to the system and data. This information should be shared with the person(s) conducting the examination of the digital media.

A forensic examiner may also discover evidence of a crime outside the scope of the search warrant. In such an event, an additional warrant should be obtained to expand the scope of the search.

See Chapter 2, Integrity, Discovery, and Disclosure of Electronic Evidence, *Digital Evidence in the Courtroom: A Guide for Law Enforcement and Prosecutors,* for further discussion (www.ojp.usdoj.gov/nij/pubs-sum/211314.htm).

Note: For a discussion of some of the issues concerning evidence collection, consult *Electronic Crime Scene Investigation: A Guide for First Responders* (www.ojp.usdoj.gov/nij/pubs-sum/187736.htm).

Reasonable accommodations

Searching the device onsite is often impractical. If the device is to be searched offsite, the investigator should consider adding language to the warrant affidavit that justifies removal.

If the device is removed for an offsite examination of the data, the examination should be completed in a timely manner. Law enforcement may consider returning copies of non-contraband seized data even if commingled with evidence of a crime to accommodate a reasonable request from suspects or third parties.

See Chapter 2, Integrity, Discovery, and Disclosure of Electronic Evidence, *Digital Evidence in the Courtroom: A Guide for Law Enforcement and Prosecutors,* for further discussion (www.ojp.usdoj.gov/nij/pubs-sum/211314.htm).

Warrantless searches

The requirement for securing a warrant has several well-recognized exceptions. Although the following is not an exhaustive list, these examples provide some idea of how the common exceptions apply to the search and seizure of digital evidence.

Consent

Consent is a valuable tool to the investigator. It can come from many sources, including a login banner, terms-of-use agreement, company policy, or a user of a shared system. Some considerations include the following:

- A computer, like a shared apartment, can have multiple users. Users may consent to a search of their private area or common areas of the computer. Additional consent may be needed if the investigator encounters password-protected files. In most cases, a parent can consent to a search of a minor child's computer.

- Consent can be limited by subject matter, duration, and other parameters. Consent can be withdrawn at any time.

- The general rule is that a private-sector employer can consent to the search of an employee's workplace computer. The rules are far more complicated when the employer is the government.

Note: For further information on consent rules, consult *Searching and Seizing Computers and Obtaining Electronic Evidence in Criminal Investigations* (www.cybercrime.gov/ s&smanual2002.htm).

Exigent circumstances

To prevent the destruction of evidence, a law enforcement agent can seize an electronic storage device. In certain cases where there is an immediate danger of losing evidence, the investigator may perform a limited search to recover or obtain the information. Once the exigent circumstances cease to exist, so does the exception.

Some evidence on pagers, cell phones, PDAs, and computers may be vulnerable to external tampering through remote access. The exigent circumstance may require the removal or isolation of the device. Once the exigency is over, the officer will need consent or a search warrant to search the device.

Search incident to arrest

The need to protect the safety of a law enforcement agent or to preserve evidence can justify a full search of an arrestee and a limited search of the arrest scene. This search incident to arrest can include a search of an electronic storage device, such as a cell phone or pager, held by the subject at the time of arrest. The search must be conducted substantially contemporaneous with the arrest. This time constraint usually means it is best to secure the device, obtain a warrant, and have the device examined by appropriate personnel.

Inventory search

The inventory search exception is intended to protect the property of a person in custody and guard against claims of damage or loss. Although untested, it is unlikely that the inventory search exception will allow a law enforcement agent to access digital evidence from a seized device without a warrant.

Plain view doctrine

The plain view exception may apply in some instances to the seizure of electronic evidence. For this exception to apply, a law enforcement agent must legitimately be in the position to see the evidence, and the incriminating nature must be immediately apparent. The plain view doctrine is best used to initially seize and secure evidence. Once the evidence has been secured, the information learned in "plain view" can be used as the basis for probable cause to obtain a search warrant.

Statutes that affect the seizure and search of electronic evidence

This section will briefly discuss several Federal statutes governing access to and disclosure of certain types of information deemed deserving of special treatment by Congress: the *Wiretap Act,* the *Pen Register and Trap and Trace Statute,* the Electronic Communications Privacy Act (ECPA), the *Privacy Protection Act (PPA),* and Communications Assistance for Law Enforcement Act of 1994 (CALEA).

> **Note:** *Searching and Seizing Computers and Obtaining Electronic Evidence in Criminal Investigations,* which provides a comprehensive analysis of Federal search-and-seizure issues and Federal privacy statutes, can be found at www.cybercrime.gov/s&smanual 2002.htm.

Omnibus Crime Control and Safe Streets Act of 1968, 18 U.S.C. § 2510 et seq. (Wiretap Act or Title III) www.usdoj.gov/criminal/cybercrime/18usc2510.htm

The Wiretap Act focuses on the interception of the content of communications while they are in transit. Examples of such interceptions include wiretapping a telephone, placing a listening device or "bug" in a room to pick up conversations, and installing keystroke loggers that capture the user's communication with a third party. The Wiretap Act also governs the disclosure of intercepted communications.

The Wiretap Act generally prohibits anyone in the United States from intercepting the contents of wire, oral, or electronic communications unless one of several exceptions applies. As a basic rule, the Wiretap Act prohibits anyone who is not a participating party to a private communication from intercepting the communication between or among the participating parties using an "electronic, mechanical, or other device," unless one of several statutory exceptions applies.

One exception includes the issuance of a court order by a court of competent jurisdiction authorizing interception. The requirements to obtain such an order are substantial.

Violation of the Wiretap Act can itself constitute a crime and may lead to civil liability. In the case of wire and oral communications (i.e., communications of the human voice), a violation may result in the suppression of evidence. To ensure compliance, initially determine whether the following apply:

■ The communication to be monitored is one of the protected communications defined in the statute.

■ The proposed surveillance constitutes an "interception" of the communication.

If both conditions are present, evaluate whether a statutory exception applies that permits the interception.

Note: Some States have versions of the Wiretap Act that are more restrictive than the Federal act. The Federal act does not preempt these laws unless Federal agents are conducting the investigation for Federal prosecution. State and local law enforcement agents must comply with any such State act, even if there is no violation of the Federal Wiretap Act.

Pen Register and Trap and Trace Statute, 18 U.S.C. § 3121 et seq. (Federal Pen/Trap Statute) www.usdoj.gov/criminal/cybercrime/pentraps3121_3127.htm

The Pen/Trap statute governs the real-time acquisition of dialing, routing, addressing, and signaling information relating to communications. Unlike the Wiretap Act, the Pen/Trap statute does not cover the acquisition of the content of communications. Rather, it covers the information about communications. A "pen register" records outgoing connection information (the telephone number dialed by the target phone), while a "trap and trace" records incoming connection information (the telephone number(s) of the device(s) calling the target phone).

The Pen/Trap statute applies not only to telephone communications, but also to Internet communications. For example, every e-mail communication contains "to" and "from" information. A pen/trap device captures such information in real time.

The Pen/Trap statute generally forbids the nonconsensual real-time acquisition of noncontent information about a wire or electronic communication unless a statutory exception applies.

Where there is no applicable exception to this prohibition, law enforcement agents must obtain a pen/trap order from the court before acquiring noncontent information (e.g., transactional, called numbers, calling numbers, signaling information) covered by the statute.

If investigators need evidence of phone calls that have already been made, they may obtain these records with a subpoena for toll records. This method is discussed in the ECPA section below.

Note: Examples of requests for Federal pen/trap orders may be found at *Searching and Seizing Computers and Obtaining Electronic Evidence in Criminal Investigations* (www.cybercrime.gov/s&smanual2002.htm). Some States have versions of the Pen/Trap statute that are more restrictive than the Federal act. The Federal act does not preempt these laws unless Federal agents conduct the investigation for Federal prosecution. State and local law enforcement agents must comply with any such State act, even if there is no violation of the Federal Pen/Trap statute.

Stored Communications, Provisions of the Electronic Communications Privacy Act, 18 U.S.C. § 2701 et seq. (ECPA) www.usdoj.gov/criminal/cybercrime/ECPA2701_2712.htm

The stored communications chapter of ECPA provides the customers and subscribers of certain communications service providers with privacy protections. This statute protects records held by providers about customers and subscribers (such as billing records), as well as files stored by the providers for customers and subscribers (such as e-mail or uploaded files). ECPA dictates what type of legal process is necessary to compel a provider to disclose specific types of customer or subscriber information to law enforcement agents. ECPA also limits what a provider may and may not voluntarily disclose to others, including the government (see Appendix D, Disclosure Rules of ECPA, for a quick reference guide to the disclosure rules of ECPA).

ECPA applies when the government seeks to obtain records about a customer or subscriber from a provider of communications services (e.g., an Internet service provider (ISP) or cellular phone provider). All information held by the provider can be compelled to be turned over through legal process, but some can also be turned over voluntarily if the provider so chooses.

ECPA applies when the government seeks to obtain copies of a customer's e-mail from an ISP. ECPA does not apply when the government seeks to obtain the same e-mail from the customer's computer.

ECPA provides that the production of some information may be compelled by subpoena, some by court order under section 2703(d) (discussed below), and some by warrant. The more sensitive the information (e.g., basic subscriber information, transactional information, or content of certain kinds of stored communications), the higher the level of legal process required to compel disclosure (e.g., subpoena, court order under 2703(d), or warrant).

As the level of government process escalates from subpoena to 2703(d) order to warrant, the information available under the less exacting standard is included at the higher level (e.g., a warrant grants access to basic subscriber information, transactional information, and content of the stored communication).

Note: Because different providers may use different terms to describe the types of data that they hold, it is advisable to consult with each provider on their preferred language when drafting the request to maximize the efficiency of obtaining the requested information.

Subscriber and Session Information: Subpoena

Under ECPA, the government may use a subpoena to obtain certain information listed in ECPA relating to the identity of a customer or subscriber, the customer or subscriber's relationship with the service provider, and basic session connection records. Specifically, a subpoena is effective to compel a service provider to disclose the following information about the customer or subscriber:

- Name.

- Address.

- Local and long-distance telephone connection records, or records of session times and durations.

- Length of service (including start date) and types of service used.

- Telephone or instrument number or other subscriber number or identity, including any temporarily assigned network address.

- The means and source of payment for such service (including any credit card or bank account number).

Notably, this list does not include extensive transaction-related records, such as logging information revealing the e-mail addresses of persons with whom a customer corresponded during prior sessions, or "buddy lists."

Other Noncontent Subscriber and Session Information: 2703(d) Order

The government will need to obtain a court order under 18 U.S.C. § 2703(d) to compel a provider to disclose more detailed records about the use of the services by a customer or subscriber. These records could include, for example:

- Account activity logs that reflect what Internet Protocol (IP) addresses the subscriber visited over time.

- E-mail addresses of others with whom the subscriber exchanged e-mail.

- "Buddy lists."

The government can also use a 2703(d) order to compel a cellular telephone service provider to turn over, in real time, records showing the cell-site location information for calls made from a subscriber's cellular phone. This information shows more of the subscriber's use of the system than that available by subpoena, but it does not include the content of the communications.

Any Federal magistrate or district court with jurisdiction over the offense under investigation may issue a 2703(d) order. State court judges authorized by the law of the State to enter orders authorizing the use of a pen/trap device may also issue 2703(d) orders. The application must offer "specific and articulable facts showing that there are reasonable grounds to believe that . . . the records or other information sought, are relevant and material to an ongoing criminal investigation." 18 U.S.C. §2703(d).

Note: In general, ECPA provides more privacy protection to the contents of communications and files stored with a provider than to records detailing the use of the service or the subscriber's identity. Refer to *Searching and Seizing Computers and Obtaining Electronic Evidence in Criminal Investigations* (www.cybercrime.gov/s&smanual 2002.htm) for examples of applications for an order under 2703(d).

Content of Stored Communications

ECPA distinguishes between communications in storage that have already been retrieved by the customer or subscriber, and those that have not. In addition, the statute distinguishes between retrieved communications that are held by a private provider (e.g., an employer who makes e-mail services available to employees and contractors only) and those held by a provider that offers its services to the public generally.

Retrieved communications held by private provider: subpoena. ECPA only applies to stored communications that a customer or subscriber has retrieved, but left on the server of the communications service provider, if the service provider offers those services to the public. If the provider does not offer those services to the public, ECPA imposes no constraints on the right of the provider to disclose such information voluntarily. ECPA does not require any heightened or particular legal process to compel disclosure of such records. For example, ECPA does not apply to a government request to an employer to produce the retrieved e-mail of a particular employee if the employer makes e-mail services and accounts available to its employees but not to the public generally. Where ECPA does not apply, such information may be available through traditional legal processes.

Note: ECPA may apply if the e-mail sought resides on the employer's server and has not yet been retrieved by the employee. In this instance, the rules discussed under Chapter 1, IV.C.3 (Search Warrant: Unretrieved Communications), of *Digital Evidence in the Courtroom: A Guide for Law Enforcement and Prosecutors* apply (www.ojp.usdoj.gov/ nij/pubs-sum/211314.htm).

Retrieved communications, unretrieved communications older than 180 days, and other files stored with a public provider: subpoena or 2703(d), with notice. ECPA does apply to stored communications that a customer or subscriber has retrieved (but left on the server of the communications service provider) if the service provider offers those services to the public. Such communications include text files, pictures, programs, or any other files that a customer may have stored on the public provider's system. Under the statute, such a provider is considered a "remote computing service" and is not permitted to voluntarily disclose such content to the government.

The government may use either a subpoena or a 2703(d) court order to compel a public service provider to disclose the contents of stored communications retrieved by a customer or subscriber. The government in either case must give prior notice of the request to the customer or subscriber.

Another provision in ECPA allows the government to delay the notice to the customer or subscriber when notice would jeopardize a pending investigation or endanger the life or physical safety of an individual. If the government uses a subpoena to compel the disclosure of stored, retrieved communications from a public service provider, the government may seek to delay notice for 90 days "upon the execution of a written certification of a supervisory official that there is reason to believe that notification of the existence of the subpoena may have an adverse result." 18 U.S.C. § 2705(a)(1)(B). The government can request extensions in 90-day increments of the original delay order. If the government uses a 2703(d) order, it may seek permission from the court to delay notice as part of the application for the order.

At the end of the delayed notice period, the government must send a copy of the request or process to the customer or subscriber, along with a letter explaining the delay.

The government may also use a subpoena with prior notice, or a 2703(d) order with prior notice, to compel a service provider to disclose communications that are unretrieved but have been on the server more than 180 days. As a practical matter, most providers will not allow unretrieved messages to stay on a server unaccessed for such a long period.

If using a search warrant or seeking noncontent information, no notice is required.

Unretrieved communications: warrant. Unretrieved communications (including voice mail) held by the provider for 180 days or fewer have the highest level of protection available under ECPA. ECPA covers such communications whether the service provider is private or public. The service provider is generally not permitted to voluntarily disclose unretrieved communications to the government.

For example, under ECPA an e-mail sent to a customer is considered unretrieved if it resides on the server of the customer's provider (i.e., an ISP or the customer's employer) waiting for the customer to log on and download the message. Once the customer downloads the e-mail (but leaves a copy on the server of the provider), the e-mail is considered retrieved. Refer to Chapter 1, IV.C.1 (Retrieved Communications Held by Private Provider) in *Digital Evidence in the Courtroom: A Guide for Law Enforcement and Prosecutors* (www.ojp.usdoj.gov/nij/pubs-sum/211314.htm), for more detail about retrieved communications.

The government may seek a warrant, such as a warrant provided by 2703(a), to compel the production of unretrieved communications in storage with a service provider. No prior notice is required to the customer or subscriber.

Note: Nonpublic providers may voluntarily disclose to the government and others subscriber and session information, transactional information, and stored communications and files without violating ECPA. Under certain circumstances, public providers may also voluntarily disclose information without violating ECPA. Some States may have applicable laws that are more restrictive than the Federal act. The Federal act does not preempt these laws unless Federal agents are conducting the investigation for Federal prosecution. State and local law enforcement agents must comply with any such State act, even if there is no violation of the Federal statute.

ECPA violation remedies

Civil damages are the exclusive remedy for violation of ECPA. Evidence seized in violation of ECPA alone will not be suppressed.

Privacy Protection Act, 42 U.S.C. § 2000aa et seq. (PPA) www.usdoj.gov/criminal/cybercrime/42usc2000aa.htm

PPA limits law enforcement's use of a search warrant to search for or seize certain materials possessed by a person for the purpose of public dissemination. These protected materials may be either "work product" (i.e., materials created by the author or publisher) or "documentary materials" (i.e., any materials that document or support the work product).

For example, a person who is creating an online newsletter may possess interview notes that could be considered "documentary materials," whereas the text of the newsletter to be published could be considered "work product" materials. PPA applies only to law enforcement actions to obtain these materials. If the material is covered by PPA, law enforcement cannot use a search warrant to obtain it.

PPA's prohibition on the use of a search warrant does not apply in any of the following circumstances:

- Materials searched for or seized are contraband, instrumentalities, or fruits of the crime.

- There is reason to believe that the immediate seizure of such materials is necessary to prevent death or serious bodily injury.

- Probable cause exists to believe that the person possessing the materials has committed or is committing a criminal offense to which the materials relate. (Except for the possession of child pornography and certain government information, this exception does not apply where the mere possession of the materials constitutes the offense.)

If evidence of a crime is commingled on a computer with PPA-protected materials, issues concerning proper scope and execution of a search warrant will arise. Recent court cases indicate that the courts are limiting the scope of PPA protection to people not suspected of committing a crime.

Civil damages are the exclusive remedy for violation of PPA. Evidence seized in violation of PPA alone will not be suppressed.

Note: For further information on PPA, consult *Searching and Seizing Computers and Obtaining Electronic Evidence in Criminal Investigations* (www.cybercrime.gov/ s&smanual2002.htm).

Privileged or Proprietary Information

In some instances, the government may have reason to believe that the place to be searched will have information that is considered "privileged" under statute or common law (e.g., when searching the office of a lawyer, doctor, or member of the clergy). Before conducting the search, the government should take care to identify the legal limitations that the jurisdiction may impose and comply with those limitations. Consider the use of taint teams, special masters, or other process as approved by the court.

- Consider in advance whether the media to be seized contain privileged or proprietary information.

- Consider obtaining a stipulation before seizing information from the target to avoid confiscating potentially privileged or proprietary information.

- Ensure that the prosecution team addresses in advance the issue of privileged or proprietary information when drafting the search warrant to avoid tainting the acquisition of evidence.

Note: For further information regarding searches involving privileged information and the use of taint teams and special masters, consult *Searching and Seizing Computers and Obtaining Electronic Evidence in Criminal Investigations* (www.cybercrime.gov/ s&smanual2002.htm).

Communications Assistance for Law Enforcement Act of 1994 (CALEA) http://www.askcalea.net/calea.html

In 1994, the Federal Government recognized that as communication systems became more complex, it would become increasingly difficult for law enforcement to perform lawful intercepts. To protect public safety and national security, the U.S. Congress enacted the Communications Assistance for Law Enforcement Act of 1994 (CALEA). CALEA further established the statutory obligation of telecommunications carriers ". . . to make clear a telecommunications carrier's duty to cooperate in the lawful interception of communications for law enforcement purposes." CALEA is codified at 47 U.S.C. §§ 1001–1021. CALEA originally required all telecommunications carriers to provide law enforcement with a CALEA connection solution. The government and the telecommunications industry are working together to develop standards for delivery of data and connection implementations for law enforcement.

Appendix A. Glossary

802.11: 802.11 refers to one of the standards developed by the Institute of Electrical and Electronics Engineers (IEEE) for wireless local area network (LAN) technology. 802.11 allows computers, printers, and other devices to communicate over a wireless LAN. For more information on the specific standards, go to www.ieee.org.

AOL Instant Messenger™ (AIM). AOL Instant Messenger™ is a popular instant messaging service provided for free by America Online. With the AIM service, instant messages can be sent over an Internet connection using the AIM software, or directly from a Web browser using AIM Express. AIM also supports file transfers, webcams, and voice conversation.

Back door: A back door is a means of access to a computer program or system that bypasses security mechanisms. Attackers often use back doors that they detect or install themselves as part of an exploit.

Banner: A login banner is an onscreen message that notifies users of the terms of access prior to allowing access to the system. A banner may indicate that system usage is subject to monitoring and disclosure.

Biometric device: Biometrics refers to technologies for measuring and analyzing human body characteristics such as fingerprints, eye retinas and irises, voice patterns, facial patterns, and hand measurements. Biometric devices are commonly used for authentication purposes and consist of a reader or scanning device and software that converts the scanned information into digital form and compares it to a known database.

BlackBerry®: A handheld device developed by RIM® that focuses on wireless e-mail communications, but can also run other applications.

Blog: Contraction for the term 'Web log." A Web-based online journal or diary that may be maintained by a user or a group.

Bluetooth®: A wireless network technology developed by the Bluetooth Special Interest Group (BSIG). Bluetooth is an open standard for short-range transmission of digital voice and data between mobile devices, desktop devices, and phones.

Body wire: A body-worn transmitter that may be hidden under clothing or disguised in another electronic device such as a pager or cell phone. The signal is transmitted to a remote receiver where it may be recorded. These devices may also include video capabilities. Body wires may be used for consensual monitoring or may require a court order.

Buddy list: Generically refers to saved lists of frequent contacts contained in instant messaging programs.

Cable modem: A modem used to connect a computer to a cable TV system that offers Internet access.

CD-ROM: (Compact Disc, Read-Only Memory) A device used to store data in a digital format. CD-ROMs are read using laser optics rather than magnetic means.

Chat logs: Computer files, usually stored on an individual's computer, that contain the content from online chat sessions. Logs can include the dates and times of communications, file transfers, and the text of the communication.

Chat programs: Software that allows communications in real time between individuals or groups of individuals and that commonly supports text messaging, file transfers, voice, video, etc. Examples of chat programs are Yahoo!®, AIM, MSN Messenger, Trillian, and PalTalk.

Chat rooms: The term referring to any number of online services where people can "chat" with each other by typing messages that are displayed almost instantly on the screens of others who are logged into the chat room.

Cloned pager: A pager that duplicates the target pager, allowing it to receive the same information as the target pager.

Communications Assistance for Law Enforcement Act of 1994 (CALEA): (47 U.S.C. §§ 1001–1021). Statute that compels communications service providers to cooperate with law enforcement in communications surveillance activities. For more information on CALEA, see www.askcalea.com.

Cradle: An accessory that connects a PDA or phone to a charger or computer and facilitates communication between the devices.

Decryption tool: Software or hardware that converts encrypted data back into its original form.

Dialed number recorder (DNR): A device connected to a line on the public switched telephone network that allows data flowing through the line to be covertly recorded and transmitted to another location. The information may include the numbers dialed, caller identification information, and content of communications.

Dialog box: A secondary window that contains buttons and various kinds of boxes through which one carries out a particular command or task. Intermediary devices, such as a security host, require a dialog box as an added layer of security between the client and remote host. In such boxes, users may provide access codes, user names, and passwords to access that host.

Digital evidence: Information stored or transmitted in binary form that may be relied on in court.

Digital subscriber line (DSL): Technology designed to allow high-speed data communication over the existing telephone lines between end-users and telephone companies.

Discussion groups: Any of a variety of online forums in which people communicate about subjects of common interest.

Domain: A network and its hardware associated with a domain name.

Domain name: A unique name registered to a specific entity for the purposes of providing a name associated with network or Internet addresses (e.g., nist.gov).

DMCA: Digital Millennium Copyright Act, 17 U.S.C. § 1201.

Dongle: Also known as a hardware key. A copy protection or licensing device supplied with software that plugs into a computer port.

Electronic communications: Any transfer of signs, signals, writing, images, sounds, data, or intelligence of any nature transmitted in whole or in part by a wire, radio, electromagnetic, photoelectronic, or photo-optical system that affects interstate or foreign commerce, but does not include—

■ Any wire or oral communication.

■ Any communication made through a tone only paging device.

■ Any communication from a tracking device.

■ Electronic funds transfer information stored by a financial institution in a communications system used for the electronic storage and transfer of funds.

Electronic Communications Privacy Act (ECPA): 18 U.S.C. §2701 et seq. ECPA regulates how the government can obtain stored account information from network service providers such as ISPs. Whenever agents or prosecutors seek stored e-mail, account records, or subscriber information from a network service provider, they must comply with ECPA. www.cybercrime.gov/cclaws.html; www.cybercrime.gov/s&smanual2002.htm#_III_.

Electronic serial number (ESN): The unique identification number embedded in a wireless phone by the manufacturer that is used to authenticate the phone with a wireless network.

E-mail header: The part of an electronic mail message or news article that precedes the body of a message and contains, among other things, the sender's name and e-mail address, IP addresses, and the date and time the message was sent.

Encoder: A device used to encode information on magnetic data stripes (e.g., driver's licenses and credit cards).

Encrypted File System (EFS): A feature of some Windows® operating systems that lets any file or folder be stored in encrypted form and decrypted only by specified users and an authorized recovery agent.

Encryption: The process of encoding data to prevent unauthorized access, especially during transmission. Encryption is usually based on one or more keys, or codes, that are essential for decoding, or returning the data to readable form.

EZPass℠: A device used for automated toll payment designed to be mounted on a vehicle, usually inside the windshield.

Faraday cage (container): (Michael Faraday, 1791–1867, British physicist.) A complete cage of metal or metallic meshwork. If a region in space is completely surrounded by a Faraday cage, ambient electromagnetic waves are effectively screened from the enclosed region, preventing radio frequency waves from ambient sources from interfering with the reception of the radiowaves emitted.

Federal Pen and Trap Statute: 18 U.S.C. § 3121 *et seq.* The statute that sets the Federal parameters under which non-content communications data can be obtained. State statutes may impose other or additional requirements.

File type: A designation of the operational or structural characteristics of a file. A file's type is often identified in the file name, usually in the file name extension.

Firewall: A combination of specialized hardware and software designed to keep unauthorized users from accessing information within a networked computer system.

FireWire: A high-speed serial bus that allows for a hot swappable connection of peripheral devices (also referred to as IEEE1394 High Performance Serial Bus).

Firmware: Software routines stored in read-only memory (ROM).

Flash media: Solid state memory device that holds digital content without power.

Floppy disk: Reusable magnetic storage media introduced in the early 1970s. It was the primary method for distributing computer software until the mid-1990s. The latest version refers to a rigid plastic cartridge measuring 3.5 inches square and about 2 millimeters thick that stores up to 1.44 megabytes (MB) of data.

Global positioning system (GPS): A navigational system involving satellites and computers that can determine the latitude, longitude, and elevation of a receiver on Earth by computing the time difference for signals from different satellites to reach the receiver.

Graphical user interface (GUI): A GUI (usually pronounced GOO-ee) is a graphical, rather than purely textual, user interface that incorporates icons, pulldown menus, and a mouse.

Header: See e-mail header.

Hidden files: Files or data that are not readily visble in a normal user interface. Many computer systems include an option to protect information from the casual user by hiding it. A cursory examination may not display hidden files, directories, or partitions to the untrained viewer. A forensic examination may be able to locate this type of information.

Hub: In a network, a device joining communications lines at a central location, providing a common connection to all devices on the network.

ICQ: (Short for I seek you). A conferencing program for the Internet that provides interactive chat and e-mail and file transfer and can alert you when someone on your predefined list has also come online. For more information on ICQ, go to www.ICQ.com.

Indented handwriting: Impressions left on underlying pages or surfaces as a result of the pressure of the handwriting. Information may be recovered through a variety of methods including using image analysis.

Instant messaging (IM): Software that allows users connected to a network (generally the Internet) to send messages to each other.

Internet Crimes Against Children (ICAC) Task Force: A U.S. Department of Justice task force that supports State and local investigations and prosecutions of Internet child exploitation. For more information, see www.icactraining.org.

Internet Protocol (IP) address: An IP address is a 32-bit binary number that uniquely identifies to other Internet hosts a host connected to the Internet, for the purposes of communication through the transfer of packets. An IP address is expressed in "dotted quad" format, consisting of the decimal values of its 4 bytes, separated with periods, for example 127.0.0.1.

Internet registries: Publicly available Internet databases containing domain registration and IP address allocation information.

Internet relay chat (IRC): Multiuser Internet chat system, where users meet in channels (rooms, virtual places, usually with a certain topic of conversation) to talk in groups or privately.

Internet service provider (ISP): An organization that provides access to the Internet.

Intrusion detection system (IDS): Hardware or software that collects network information that may reveal indicators of illicit network activity.

Jaz®: A high-capacity removable hard disk system manufactured by Iomega Corporation.

Key: In encryption and digital signatures, an alphanumeric code used for encrypting and decrypting information.

Keystroke monitoring: Hardware or software that is used to log individual keystrokes typed on a keyboard. These monitors are typically concealed and may be difficult to detect by the user.

Logical file copy: A logical file copy is the process of copying files from one location to another. This is the copy process most computer users are familiar with. During the process, only the content of the file is copied and, depending on the program and operating system used to copy the file, some metadata may be retained. The logical file copy does not copy any slack, deleted, or other areas of the media not normally seen by the operating system (as opposed to physical copy or imaging).

Login (Log In): To gain access to a specific computer, program, or network by identifying oneself, typically with a user name and a password.

LoJack®: A private security system that assists law enforcement by locating stolen vehicles. Consists of a small radio frequency transceiver hidden on a vehicle and radio tracking devices used by law enforcement.

Memory card: A memory module that is used to extend RAM storage capacity or in place of a hard disk in a portable computer, such as a laptop or handheld PC. The module is usually the size of a credit card and can be plugged into a PCMCIA-compliant portable computer.

Metadata: A description or definition of electronic data or data that describes other data (data about data). Often, metadata can only be accessed in certain viewing modes. Metadata can include descriptive HTML tags and information about when a document was created, and what changes have been made on that document.

Microdrive: One-inch disk drives introduced in 1998 by IBM. The microdrive is designed for use in handheld computers and special purpose devices such as digital cameras and wireless telephones.

Minimization: The legal requirement to restrict the monitoring of communications that fall outside the scope of the relevant court order.

MP3 player: A portable device designed to play MP3 (MPEG Audio Layer 3) audio files. Other types of computer files can be stored on MP3 players.

Multiplex: A technique used in video capture and transmission to enable a number of separate signals (analog or digital) to be sent or stored simultaneously over a single line or channel. Separate signals include camera information and could also include time or date. This process enables the data from several cameras to be stored on the same tape or device, and when demultiplexed, can be viewed individually or in aggregate.

Network: A group of computers or devices connected to one another to share information and resources.

Network packet: A bundle of data that is routed between an origin and destination on a network. The bundle of data sent over a network is divided into efficiently sized packets for routing. Each of these packets includes the address of the destination. Upon arrival at the destination, the packets are reassembled into their original form.

Newsgroup: Worldwide distributed computer bulletin board system arranged by topic, such as rec.pets.cats or alt.internet.services.

Offsite storage: The storing of data at a physical location other than where the user is located. Companies may use offsite storage to store their backup copies of data for protection. When used in reference to the Internet, offsite storage may also mean data that are stored on a file server at a different location than the user.

Online chat: See chat rooms.

OnStar®: A vehicle navigation system with tracking and emergency services.

Operating system: The master control program that runs a computer. Provides an interface between the computer hardware and software. Popular operating systems include Windows®, MacOS, Unix®, and Linux.

Optical media: A direct access disk that is read and may be written by light.

Parabolic microphone: A dish-shaped microphone designed to concentrate and amplify sounds received from a distance.

Passphrase (password): A group of characters used to serve as a security measure against unauthorized access to data. These may be in the form of a group of unrelated characters, words, or phrases.

Passphrase protection: Many software programs include the ability to protect a file using a password. One type of password protection is sometimes called "access denial." If this feature is used, the data will be present on the disk in the normal manner, but the software program will not open or display the file without the user entering the password. Another type of password protection may include encryption.

PayPal®: An online payment company that allows for secure transactions when paying for goods or services.

Peer to peer (P2P): A communications network that allows all workstations and computers to act as servers to each other.

Pen Register and Trap and Trace Statute: See Federal Pen and Trap Statute.

Personal digital assistant (PDA): A PDA refers to any small handheld device that provides computing and data storage capabilities. Examples of PDAs include the PalmPilot® and the BlackBerry®.

Personal Computer Memory Card Interface Association (PCMCIA): Commonly referred to as PC cards. A specification for credit card-sized removable modules for portable computers. PCMCIA devices may be used for network adaptors, sound cards, radio receivers, storage devices, etc.

Platform: As related to video, refers to the specific type of hardware or software used to create the video image.

Port: As related to TCP/IP, a software-created access point—a "logical connection place"—for moving information to and out of a computer. Each communication service on a computer (e.g., FTP, e-mail, Web) is assigned a port number. Ports are numbered from 0 to 65535. Ports 0 to 1024 are reserved for use by certain privileged services (e.g., http is assigned port number 80).

PPA: Privacy Protection Act - 42 U.S.C. § 2000aa *et seq.*

Preservation order: Request authorized under 18 U.S.C. § 2703(f) requiring an electronic communications service provider or remote computing service to preserve certain types of information for a period of 90 days.

Pretty Good Privacy (PGP): A dual key (public/private) encryption program. Properly used, PGP is very difficult to break. Many will argue it is impossible to break using today's techniques.

Random access memory (RAM): A computer's short-term memory that provides memory space for the computer to work with data. Information stored in the RAM is lost when the computer is turned off. A computer with 128 MB RAM has approximately 128 million bytes of memory available. Contrast to read only memory, which is used to store programs that start a computer and do diagnostics.

Read only memory (ROM): A memory chip that permanently stores instructions and data.

Registrar: Entity authorized to register domain names for registrants.

Remote data storage: Storage of data in a location other than the physical location of the device. This may be through a local network or over the Internet. See offsite storage.

Router: A device that routes data from one local area network or wide area network to another. A router receives transmitted messages and forwards them to their correct destinations over the most efficient available route.

Search engine: Software that searches for data based on specific criteria. On the Internet, it is a Web site or program that uses keywords to search for documents found on the World Wide Web, newsgroups, and FTP archives (e.g., Google™).

Shareware: A software distribution plan that allows a user to sample software without cost, usually on a limited time or functionality basis. This is in contrast to freeware, which has no such limitations to use.

Sleep mode: This state is reached by a timer, which is triggered after a period of inactivity. This mode allows battery life to be preserved by dimming the display and taking other appropriate actions.

Smart card: A credit card with a built-in microprocessor and memory used for identification or financial transactions. When inserted into a reader, it transfers data to and from a central computer. It is more secure than a magnetic stripe card and can be programmed to self-destruct if the wrong password is entered too many times.

Sniffer: Software that monitors network packets and can be used to intercept data, including, for example, passwords and credit card numbers.

Spamming: The same article (or essentially the same article) posted an unacceptably high number of times to one or more news groups. Spam is also uninvited e-mail sent to many people or unsolicited e-mail advertising.

Steganography: From the Greek, this term means "hidden writing." It is the process of concealing data within a different type of file. This concealed data may be encrypted prior to the concealment. This is accomplished by means of a software program, and the carrier files are frequently image files in the GIF format, video files in the MPEG format, and audio files in the WAV format.

Subscriber Identity Module (SIM): A small chip installed in a wireless telephone that stores user and network information.

Synchronized: Protocols that allow users to view, modify, and transfer or update PDA data from the PC or vice versa. The two most common synchronization protocols are Microsoft's ActiveSync and Palm's HotSync.

System administrator: The individual who has legitimate supervisory rights over a computer system. The administrator maintains the highest access to the system. Also can be known as sysop, sysadmin, and system operator.

Three-track reader: A device that reads and records multiple tracks on a magnetic stripe from a single card (e.g., credit cards, magnetically encoded driver's licenses, health care cards, password entry, fitness club cards).

ThumbDrive®: Combines flash memory technologies with USB connection to create a self-contained drive and media package the size of a thumb. It plugs directly into the USB port of any computer and can store virtually any digital data.

Title III: Part of ECPA, 18 U.S.C. § 2510 *et seq.*

TiVo®: TiVo works with any TV setup, from a simple antenna to cable, digital cable, and satellite, to automatically find and digitally record up to 140 hours.

Trojan: A program that comes in secretly and quietly but carries a destructive payload. Once a computer becomes infected by the worm or virus that the Trojan carries into a computer, repairing the damage can be very difficult. Trojans often carry programs that allow someone else to have total and complete access to a computer. Trojans usually come attached to another file, such as an .avi or .exe, or even a .jpg (www.ircbeginner.com/ircinfo/ircglossary. html).

Universal Serial Bus (USB) drive or device: USB is known as a plug-and-play interface between a computer and a peripheral, such as a mouse, keyboard, digital camera, printer, or scanner. Unlike devices connected via SCSI ports, USB devices can be added to and removed from the computer without having to reboot the computer (http://practice. findlaw.com/glossary.html).

Voice over Internet Protocol (Voice over IP/VoIP): The practice of using packet-based networks instead of the standard public switched telephone network to send voice data (www.voxpilot.com).

Voice over the Internet Protocol is a term used in IP telephony for a set of facilities that manages the delivery of voice information using IP. In general, this means sending voice information in digital form in discrete packets rather than in the traditional circuit-committed protocols of the public switched telephone network (PSTN). A major advantage of VoIP and Internet telephony is that they avoid the tolls charged by ordinary telephone service.

Volatility/volatile memory: Memory that loses its content when power is turned off or lost.

Wardriving: The process of driving around in a car in an attempt to identify an open wireless network

Waypoint: Geographic coordinate used for navigation.

Webcam: A camera connected to a computer that captures digital images for transmission over a network.

WebTV®: A proprietary device and service that provides an Internet access console for use with a standard television and may or may not contain data storage.

Wire communication: Any aural transfer made in whole or in part through the use of facilities for the transmission of communications by the aid of wire, cable, or other like connection. The transfer is between the point of origin and the point of reception (including the use of such connection in a switching station) and is furnished or operated by any person engaged in providing or operating such facilities for the transfer of interstate or foreign communications or communications affecting interstate or foreign commerce. Wire communication also includes any electronic storage of such communication.

Wireless hotspot: Hotspot provides high-speed wireless Internet access in public locations.

Wiretap Act: Title III of ECPA, 18 U.S.C. § 2510 *et seq.*

Write protection: The setting of an audio, video, data tape, hard drive, diskette, or other magnetic medium to prevent accidental overwriting or erasure by recording or storing data over it. Also refers to software or hardware that is designed to prevent inadvertent writing to a hard drive or other magnetic medium. Write protection should be used when imaging suspect drives.

Zip® disk: A 3.5-inch removable disk drive. The drive is bundled with software that can catalog disks and lock the files for security.

Appendix B. Technical Resources List

The U.S. Department of Justice has created the Computer and Telecommunication Coordinator (CTC) Program. Each U.S. Attorney's Office (USAO) has designated at least one CTC. For information, visit www.usdoj.gov/crimina/cybercrime/chips.html.

Regional Computer Forensic Laboratory (RCFL) Contacts

Regional Computer Forensic Laboratory National Program Office
Engineering Research Facility
Attn: RCFL National Program Office
Building 27958–A
Quantico, VA 22135
Phone: 703–902–5502
E-mail: info@nationalrcfl.org
www.rcfl.gov

Chicago RCFL Office
610 South Canal Street
Chicago, IL 60607
Phone: 312–913–9270
Fax: 312–913–9408
www.chicagorcfl.org/

Greater Houston RCFL Office
2900 North Loop West, Ninth Floor
Houston, TX 77092
Phone: 713–316–7878
www.ghrcfl.org/

Heart of America RCFL Office
4150 North Mulberry Drive, Suite 250
Kansas City, MO 64116-1696
Phone: 816–584–4300
www.harcfl.org/

Intermountain West RCFL Office
257 East 200 South, Suite 1200
Salt Lake City, UT 84111
Phone: 801–579–1400
www.iwrcfl.org/

Miami Valley RCFL Office
Federal Building
200 West Second Street
Dayton, OH 45402
Phone: 937–512–1913
Fax: 937–512–1950
www.mvrcfl.org/

New Jersey RCFL Office
NJSP Technology Center
1200 Negron Drive
Hamilton, NJ 08691
Phone: 609–584–5051, ext. 5676
www.njrcfl.org/

North Texas RCFL Office
301 North Market Street, #500
Dallas, TX 75202-1878
Phone: 972–559–5800
Fax: 972–559–5880
www.ntrcfl.org/

Northwest RCFL Office
1201 Northeast Lloyd Boulevard, Suite 600
Portland, OR 97237
Phone: 503–224–4181
www.nwrcfl.org/

Rocky Mountain RCFL Office
1961 Stout Street, Suite 1823
Denver, CO 80294
Phone: 303–629–7171
www.rmrcfl.org/

San Diego RCFL Office
9737 Aero Drive (street address)
San Diego, CA 92123
9797 Aero Drive (mailing address)
San Diego, CA 92123
Phone: 858–499–7799
Fax: 858–499–7798
E-mail: rcfl@rcfl.org
www.sdrcfl.org/

Silicon Valley RCFL Office
4600 Bohannon Drive, Suite 200
Menlo Park, CA 94025
Phone: 408–795–4314
www.svrcfl.org/

Internet Crimes Against Children Regional Task Forces

The Internet Crimes Against Children (ICAC) Task Force Program helps State and local law enforcement agencies develop an effective response to cyber enticement and child pornography cases. This help encompasses forensic and investigative components, training and technical assistance, victim services, and community education. Numerous task forces have been established throughout the Nation.

The ICAC Program was developed in response to the increasing number of children and teenagers using the Internet, the proliferation of child pornography, and the heightened online activity by predators searching for unsupervised contact with underage victims. The FY 1998 Justice Appropriations Act (Pub. L. No. 105–119) directed the Office of Juvenile Justice and Delinquency Prevention (OJJDP) to create a national network of State and local law enforcement cyber units to investigate cases of child sexual exploitation (i.e., ICAC).

Listed below by State are agencies and departments involved in the ICAC Program.

Alabama

Alabama Bureau of Investigation
3402 Demetropolis Road
Mobile, AL 36693
Phone: 251–660–2350
www.dps.state.al.us/public/abi/icac

Arizona

Phoenix Police Department
620 West Washington Street
Phoenix, AZ 85003
Phone: 602–495–0483
www.phoenix.gov/police

Akansas

Arkansas State Police
#1 State Police Plaza Drive
Little Rock, AR 72209
Phone: 501–618–8386
www.asp.state.ar.us

California

Los Angeles Police Department
150 North Los Angeles Street, Room 136
Los Angeles, CA 90012
Phone: 213–485–2883
www.lapdonline.org

Sacramento County Sheriff's Office
711 G Street
Sacramento, CA 95814
Phone: 916–874–3030
www.sachitechcops.org

San Diego Police Department
9630 Aero Drive
San Diego, CA 92123
Phone: 858–573–0689
E-mail: sdicac@sdicac.org
www.sdicac.org/

San Jose Police Department
201 West Mission Street
San Jose, CA 95110
Phone: 408–277–4102
E-mail: info@svicac.org
www.svicac.org/

Colorado

Colorado Springs Police Department
705 South Nevada Avenue
Colorado Springs, CO 80903
Phone: 719–444–7541
www.springsgov.com/Page.asp?
 NavID=1480

Connecticut

Connecticut State Police
278 Colony Street
Meriden, CT 06451
Phone: 203–639–6492
www.state.ct.us/dps/DSS/
 ComputerCrimes.htm

District of Columbia

Office of Juvenile Justice and Delinquency Prevention
810 Seventh Street N.W.
Washington, DC 20001
Phone: 202–616–7323
www.ojp.usdoj.gov/ojjdp

Florida

Broward County Sheriff's Office
2601 West Broward Boulevard
Ft. Lauderdale, FL 33312
Phone: 954–888–5256
E-mail: leachtaskforce@sheriff.org
www.sheriff.org

Gainesville Police Department
P.O. Box 1250
721 North West Sixth Street
Gainesville, FL 32602
Phone: 352–334–2561
www.gainesvillepd.org

Georgia

Georgia Bureau of Investigation
3121 Panthersville Road
Decatur, GA 30034
Phone: 404–212–4050
www.ganet.org/gbi

Hawaii

Hawaii Department of the Attorney General
235 South Beretania Street, 16th Floor
Honolulu, HI 96813
Phone: 808–587–4114
E-mail: atg_icac@hawaii.gov
www.hawaii.gov/ag/hicac/index.htm

Indiana

Indiana State Police
Government Center North
100 North Senate, Room 314
Indianapolis, IN 46204
Phone: 317–247–1852
www.in.gov/isp/bci/criminal/
 special.html

Kansas

Sedgwick County Sheriff's Office
130 South Market
Wichita, KS 67202
Phone: 316–337–6562
www.sedgwickcounty.org/emcu

Kentucky

Kentucky State Police
1240 Airport Road
Frankfort, KY 40601
Phone: 502–226–2160
www.kentuckystatepolice.org

Louisiana

Louisiana Department of Justice
339 Florida Street, Suite 402
Baton Rouge, LA 70801
Phone: 225–342–0921
www.ag.state.la.us/icac.aspx

Maryland

Maryland State Police
7155 Columbia Gateway Drive
Columbia, MD 21046
Phone: 410–977–4519
E-mail: icac@mdsp.org
http://icac.mdsp.org

Massachusetts

Massachusetts State Police
340 West Brookfield Road
New Braintree, MA 01531
Phone: 508–867–1080

Michigan

Michigan State Police
4000 Collins Road
Lansing, MI 48909
Phone: 517–336–6444
www.michigan.gov/ag/0,1607,7-123-
1589_35832_35837-142194—00.html

Minnesota

St. Paul Police Department
367 Grove Street, Second Floor
St. Paul, MN 55101
Phone: 651–266–5882
E-mail: micac@ci.stpaul.mn.us
www.ci.stpaul.mn.us/depts/police/
   icac/icac.html

Missouri

**St. Louis Metropolitan Police
Department**
1200 Clark
St. Louis, MO 63101
Phone: 314–444–5441
stlcin.missouri.org/circuit attorney/
   sexcrimes.cfm

Nebraska

Nebraska State Patrol
4411 South 108th Street
Omaha, NE 68137
Phone: 402–595–2410
www.nsp.state.ne.us/findfile.asp?id2=52

Nevada

**Las Vegas Metropolitan Police
Department**
3010 West Charleston, #120
Las Vegas, NV 89102
Phone: 702–229–3599
www.lvmpd.com

New Hampshire

**Office of Juvenile Justice and
Delinquency Prevention ICAC Task Force
Training and Technical Assistance**
University of New Hampshire
Crimes Against Children Research Center,
   West Edge
7 Leavitt Lane
Durham, NH 03824
Phone: 603–862–7031
www.unh.edu/ccrc/NJOV_info_page.htm

Portsmouth Police Department
3 Junkins Avenue
Portsmouth, NH 03801
Phone: 603–427–1500
www.ci.keene.nh.us/police/task_force.htm

New Jersey

New Jersey State Police
P.O. Box 7068
West Trenton, NJ 08628
Phone: 609–822–2000
www.njsp.org

New York

New York State Police
1220 Washington Avenue, Building 30
Albany, NY 12226-3000
Phone: 518–457–5712
www.troopers.state.ny.us/Criminal_
Investigation/Internet_Crimes_Against_
Children

North Carolina

North Carolina Bureau of Investigation
P.O. Box 25099
Raleigh, NC 27611
Phone: 919–716–0000
www.ncsbi.gov/icac/icap.jsp

Ohio

Cuyahoga County Prosecutor's Office
1200 Ontario Street, Ninth Floor
Cleveland, OH 44115
Phone: 216–443–7825
http://prosecutor.cuyahogacounty.us

Oklahoma

**Oklahoma State Bureau of
Investigation**
6600 North Harvey
Oklahoma City, OK 73116
Phone: 405–848–6724
www.osbi.state.ok.us

Pennsylvania

**Delaware County District Attorney's
Office**
Media Courthouse CID
Media, PA 19063
Phone: 610–891–4709
www.delcoicac.com/home.html

South Carolina

**South Carolina Attorney General's
Office**
P.O. Box 11549
Columbia, SC 29211
Phone: 803–734–6151
E-mail: info@sckidsonline.com
www.sckidsonline.com

Tennessee

Knoxville Police Department
800 Howard Baker, Jr. Avenue
Knoxville, TN 37915
Phone: 865–215–7020
www.ci.knoxville.tn.us/kpd/
crimesvschildren.asp

Texas

Dallas Police Department
Child Exploitation Unit
1400 South Lamar Street, Room 3N061
Dallas, TX 75215
Phone: 214–671–4211
www.dallaspolice.net/index.cfm?
page_ID=3114

Utah

Utah Office of Attorney General
257E 200 South, Suite 1200
Salt Lake City, UT 84111
Phone: 801–579–4530
http://attorneygeneral.utah.gov/ICAC/
icacmain.htm

Virginia

Bedford County Sheriff's Office
1345 Falling Creek Road
Bedford, VA 24523
Phone: 540–586–4800
www.blueridgethunder.com

National Center for Missing & Exploited Children
699 Prince Street
Alexandria, VA 22314
Phone: 703–837–6337
www.missingkids.com

Washington

Seattle Police Department
610 Fifth Avenue
Seattle, WA 98104
Phone: 206–684–4351
www.cityofseattle.net/police/Programs/
    ICAC/icac.htm

Wisconsin

Wisconsin Department of Justice
17 West Main Street
Madison, WI 53702
Phone: 608–267–1326
www.doj.state.wi.us/dci/tech/#internet

Wyoming

Wyoming Division of Criminal Investigation
316 West 22nd Street
Cheyenne, WY 82002
Phone: 307–777–7806
http://wyomingicac.net

State Contacts

National Association of Attorneys General (NAAG) Computer Crime Contact List

NAAG
750 First Street N.E., Suite 1100
Washington, DC 20002
Phone: 202–326–6000

Alabama

Office of the Attorney General
Public Corruption and White Collar Crime
    Division
11 South Union Street
Montgomery, AL 36113
Phone: 334–353–8494

Alaska

Office of the Attorney General
Special Prosecutions and Appeals
310 K Street, Suite 308
Anchorage, AK 99501–2064
Phone: 907–269–6250

Arizona

Maricopa County Attorney's Office
Technology and Electronic Crimes Bureau
301 West Jefferson Street, Fifth Floor
Phoenix, AZ 85003
Phone: 602–506–0139

Office of the Attorney General
Special Investigation Section
1275 West Washington Street
Phoenix, AZ 85007
Phone: 602–542–4266

Office of the Attorney General
Technology Crimes Unit
1275 West Washington Street
Phoenix, AZ 85007
Phone: 602–542–3881
E-mail: aginquiries@ag.state.az.us

Arkansas

Office of the Attorney General
Consumer Protection Division
323 Center Street, Suite 200
Little Rock, AR 72201
Phone: 501–682–2007

California

California Bureau of Investigation
3046 Prospect Park Drive, Unit 1
Rancho Cordova, CA 95760
Phone: 916–464–2001

Office of the Attorney General
California Department of Justice
1300 I Street, Suite 1101
Sacramento, CA 94244-2550
Phone: 916–445–9555

Office of the Attorney General
California Department of Justice
455 Golden Gate, Suite 11000
San Francisco, CA 94102
Phone: 415–703–1372
(Supports the REACT task force in Santa
Clara County/Silicon Valley)

Office of the Attorney General
California Department of Justice
455 Golden Gate, Suite 11000
San Francisco, CA 94102
Phone: 415–803–5868
(Supports the North Bay Task Force
covering the San Francisco Bay area)

Office of the Attorney General
California Department of Justice
110 West A Street, Suite 1100
San Diego, CA 92101
Phone: 619–645–2823
(Supports the San Diego Regional Task
Force and RCFL)

Colorado

Colorado Bureau of Investigation
Colorado Department of Public Safety
690 Kipling Street, Suite 3000
Denver, CO 80215
Phone: 303–239–4292

**Colorado Internet Crimes Against
Children Task Force**
Pueblo High Tech Crime Unit
Pueblo County Sheriff's Office
320 South Joe Martinez Boulevard
Pueblo West, CO 81007
Phone: 719–583–4736

Denver District Attorney's Office
303 West Colfax Avenue, #1300
Denver, CO 80204
Phone: 720–913-9000

Denver Police Department
Computer Crimes Investigations Unit
1331 Cherokee Street
Denver, CO 80204
Phone: 720–913–6168

Connecticut

Connecticut State Police
Computer Crimes and Electronic
    Evidence Unit
278 Colony Street
Meriden, CT 06451
Phone: 203–639–6492

Office of the Chief State's Attorney
300 Corporate Place
Rocky Hill, CT 06067
Phone: 860–258–5800

Delaware

Delaware State Police
High Technology Crimes Unit
1575 McKee Road, Suite 204
Dover, DE 19904
Phone: 302–739–2467

Office of the Attorney General
Criminal Division
820 North French Street, Seventh Floor
Wilmington, DE 19801
Phone: 302–577–8500

District of Columbia

Office of the Attorney General for the District of Columbia
441 Fourth Street N.W., Suite 1060N
Washington, DC 20001
Phone: 202–727–6253

Florida

Florida Department of Law Enforcement
Computer Crime Center
P.O. Box 1489
Tallahassee, FL 32302
Phone: 850–410–7060

Office of the Statewide Prosecution
135 West Central Boulevard, Suite 1000
Orlando, FL 32807
Phone: 904–245–0893

Georgia

Georgia Bureau of Investigation
5255 Snapfinger Park Drive, Suite 150
Decatur, GA 30035
Phone: 770–987–2323
www.ganet.org/gbi

Office of the Attorney General
40 Capital Square
135 State Judicial Building
Atlanta, GA 30334–1300
Phone: 404–656–5959

Hawaii

Department of the Attorney General
425 Queen Street
Honolulu, HI 96813
Phone: 808–586–1160/808–586–1240

Idaho

Office of the Attorney General
Criminal Division
700 West Jefferson Street, Room 210
Boise, ID 83720
Phone: 208–332–3096

Illinois

Cook County State's Attorney's Office
2650 South California
Room 13 B 30
Chicago, IL 60608
Phone: 773–869–2728

Office of the Attorney General
High Tech Crimes Bureau
Illinois Computer Crime Institute
100 West Randolph Street, 12th Floor
Chicago, IL 60601
Phone: 312–814–3762

Indiana

Marion Police Department
Computer Crime Investigations and
    Forensic Lab
301 South Branson Street
Marion, IN 46952
Phone: 765–662–9981

Office of the Indiana Attorney General
Internet Fraud—Consumer Protection
    Division
Phone: 317–232–6300

Iowa

Office of the Attorney General
1305 East Walnut Street
Des Moines, IA 50319
Phone: 515–281–5164

Kansas

Office of the Attorney General
Kansas Bureau of Investigation
High Tech Crime Investigation Unit
1620 S.W. Tyler
Topeka, KS 66612
Phone: 785–296–8200

Kentucky

Office of the Attorney General
Special Prosecutions Division
1024 Capitol Center Drive
Frankfort, KY 40601
Phone: 502–696–5337

Louisiana

Office of the Attorney General
High Tech Crimes Unit
P.O. Box 94095
Baton Rouge, LA 70804
Phone: 225–342–7552

Maine

Maine Computer Crimes Task Force
171 Park Street
Lewiston, ME 04240
Phone: 207–784–2384

Maine Computer Crimes Task Force
15 Oak Grove Road
Vassalboro, Maine 04989
Phone: 207–877–8081

Office of the Attorney General
Computer Crimes Task Force
44 Oak Street, Fourth Floor
Portland, ME 04101
Phone: 207–626–8800

Maryland

Maryland State Police
Computer Crimes Unit
7155 Columbia Gateway Drive
Columbia, MD 21046
Phone: 410–290–1620

Office of the Attorney General
Criminal Investigations Division
200 South Paul Place
Baltimore, MD 21202
Phone: 410–576–6380

Massachusetts

Office of the Attorney General
High Tech and Computer Crimes Division
One Ashburton Place
Boston, MA 02108–1698
Phone: 617–727–2200

Michigan

Department of the Attorney General
High Tech Crime Unit
18050 Deering
Livonia, MI 48152
Phone: 734–525–4151

Minnesota

Department of Public Safety
Bureau of Criminal Apprehension
1246 University
St. Paul, MN 55104–4197
Phone: 651–642–0610

Office of the Attorney General
Criminal Division
525 Park Street, Suite 500
St. Paul, MN 55103
Phone: 651–297–1050

Mississippi

Office of the Attorney General
Public Integrity Section
P.O. Box 2
Jackson, MS 39205
Phone: 601–359–4250

Missouri

Office of the Attorney General
High Tech Crime Unit
3100 Broadway Street, #609
Kansas City, MO 64111
Phone: 816–889–5000

Office of the Attorney General
High Tech Crime Unit
1530 Rax Court
Jefferson City, MO 65109
Phone: 816–889–5000

Montana

Office of the Attorney General
Legal Services Division
215 North Sanders
Helena, MT 59620
Phone: 406–444–2026

Office of the Attorney General
Computer Crime Unit
303 North Roberts, Room 361
Helena, MT 59620
Phone: 406–444–3875

Nebraska

Nebraska State Patrol
Internet Crimes Against Children Unit
4411 South 108 Street
Omaha, NE 68137
Phone: 402–595–2410

Nevada

Office of the Attorney General
Nevada Cyber Crime Task Force
5420 Kietzke Lane, Suite 202
Reno, NV 89511
Phone: 775–688–1818

New Hampshire

Office of the Attorney General
33 Capitol Street
Concord, NH 03301–6397
Phone: 603–271–3671

New Jersey

Office of the Attorney General
Computer Analysis and Tech Unit
25 Market Street
P.O. Box 085
Trenton, NJ 08625–0085
Phone: 609–984–6500

New Jersey State Police
High Tech Crime Unit
P.O. Box 7068
West Trenton, NJ 08628
Phone: 609–882–2000, ext. 2904

New Mexico

Office of the Attorney General
Special Prosecutions Division
P.O. Drawer 1508
Sante Fe, NM 87504–1508
Phone: 505–827–6000

New York

Erie County Sheriff's Office
Computer Crime Unit
10 Delaware Avenue
Buffalo, NY 14202-3473
Phone: 716–662–6150

New York Police Department
Computer Investigation and
 Technology Unit
One Police Plaza
New York, NY 10038
Phone: 646–610–5397
E-mail: citu@nypd.org

Office of the Attorney General
Criminal Prosecutions Bureau
Statler Towers
107 Delaware Avenue
Buffalo, NY 14202–3473
Phone: 716–853–8400

North Carolina

North Carolina State Bureau of Investigation
Financial Crimes
P.O. Box 629
Raleigh, NC 27602
Phone: 919–716–0000

Office of the Attorney General
Law Enforcement and Prosecution
   Division
P.O. Box 629
Raleigh, NC 27602
Phone: 919–716–6500

North Dakota

Office of the Attorney General
Bureau of Criminal Investigation
Cybercrime Unit
P.O. Box 1054
Bismark, ND 58502–1044
Phone: 701–328–5500

Office of the Attorney General
Criminal and Regulatory Division
600 East Boulevard Avenue, 17th Floor
Bismarck, ND 58505
Phone: 701–328–2210

Ohio

Hamilton County Sheriff's Office
Regional Electronics and Computer
Investigations Task Force
1000 Sycamore Street
Cincinnati, OH 45202
Phone: 513–946–6687/6688

Office of the Attorney General
Computer Crime Task Force
140 East Town Street, 14th Floor
Columbus, OH 43215–6001
Phone: 614–644–7233

Office of the Attorney General
Computer Crime Unit
1560 State Route 56
London, OH 43140
Phone: 740–845–2000

Oklahoma

Office of the Attorney General
Consumer Protection Division
4545 North Lincoln Boulevard, Suite 260
Oklahoma City, OK 73105
Phone: 405–521–4274

Oregon

Eugene Police Department
Financial Crimes Unit
777 Pearl Street, Room 107
Eugene OR 97401
Phone: 541–682–2682

Pennsylvania

Erie County District Attorney's Office
Erie County Court House
140 West Sixth Street
Erie, PA 16501
Phone: 814–451–7023

Office of Attorney General
Computer Forensics Section
2490 Boulevard of the Generals
Norristown, PA 19403
Phone: 610–631–5937

Office of the Attorney General
Computer Forensics Unit
106 Lowthar Street
Lemoyne, PA 17043
Phone: 717–712–2023

Office of the District Attorney
Delaware County Courthouse and
   Government Center
201 West Front Street
Media, PA 19063
Phone: 610–891–4292

Pennsylvania State Police
Computer Crimes Unit
1800 Elmerton Avenue
Harrisburg, PA 17110
Phone: 717–772–5116

Rhode Island

Department of the Attorney General
Criminal Division
150 South Main Street
Providence, RI 02903
Phone: 401–274–4400

South Carolina

Office of the Attorney General
Criminal Division
620 North Main Street, Suite 201
Greenville, SC 29601
Phone: 803–734–3970

State Law Enforcement Division
Computer Crimes Unit
P.O. Box 21398
Colombia, SC 29221–1398
Phone: 803–896–2277

South Dakota

Office of the Attorney General
1302 East Highway 14
Suite One
Pierre, SD 57501–8501
Phone: 605–773–3215

Office of the Attorney General
Criminal Division
Box 70
Robin City, SD 57709
Phone: 605–394–2258

Tennessee

Office of the Attorney General
Enforcement Division
425 Fifth Avenue, North
Nashville, TN 37243
Phone: 615–741–3491

Texas

Office of the Attorney General
Internet Bureau
P.O. Box 12548
Austin, TX 78711–2548
Phone: 512–936–2899

Utah

Office of the Attorney General
Criminal Division
P.O. Box 140814
Salt Lake City, UT 84102
Phone: 801–531–5380

Office of the Attorney General
Investigation Division
236 State Capital
Salt Lake City, UT 84114–0854
Phone: 801–538–9600

Vermont

**Chittenden Unit for Special
Investigations**
Internet Crimes Against Children
    Task Force
50 Cherry Street, Suite 102
Burlington, VT 05401
Phone: 802–652–6800

Office of the Attorney General
109 State Street
Montpelier, VT 05609–1001
Phone: 802–828–5512

Virginia

Office of the Attorney General
Computer Crimes Unit
900 East Main Street
Richmond, VA 23219
Phone: 804–659–3122
E-mail: Cybercrime@oag.state.va.us

Virginia State Police
High Tech Crimes Unit
P.O. Box 27472
Richmond, VA 23261
Phone: 804–674–2000

Washington

Oak Harbor Police Department
860 S.E. Barrington Drive
Oak Harbor, WA 98277
Phone: 360–679–5551

Office of the Attorney General
High Tech Crimes Unit
900 Fourth Avenue, Suite 2000
Seattle, WA 98164
Phone: 206–464–6430

West Virginia

Not available.

Wisconsin

Wisconsin Department of Justice
Criminal Litigation, Antitrust, Consumer
    Protection, and Public Integrity Unit and
    the Computer Crimes Unit
P.O. Box 7857
123 West Washington Avenue
Madison, WI 53707-78957
Phone: 608–266–1221/608–266–1671

Wyoming

Office of the Attorney General
123 Capitol Building
200 West 24th Street
Cheyenne, WY 82002
Phone: 307–777–7841

Office of the Attorney General
Division of Criminal Investigation
16 West 22nd Street
Cheyenne, WY 82002
Phone: 307–777–7181

Appendix C. Hacked Devices

Items found during the course of an investigation may not always be used for their intended purpose. A device that has been modified to perform an unintended function is referred to as a "hacked device." Hacking a device may involve reconfiguring, programming, or otherwise tampering with its original infrastructure. Hacked devices may not be easily distinguishable from their original forms. Investigators should also be aware that innocuous looking devices may be used as camouflage (e.g., removing the components of a device and using the case to disguise another device's components).

Recently, it has become popular to hack gaming consoles, which are actually stripped down computers with an emphasis on graphics capabilities. Companies of ten produce gaming consoles at a loss, counting on making up the revenue through sales of games. People who desire inexpensive computers can buy a gaming console, download any of several manuals that have been released on how to load a standard operating system, and make the necessary alterations. This process creates a portable, fully functional computer that could be used to perform a network intrusion or to store contraband graphics files. An investigator who is unaware of the existence of hacked devices might seize only "traditional" computers during a seizure and leave the real evidence behind.

Other examples:

- TiVo® and WebTV® have hard drives that may contain evidence not related to their main function of archiving television content.

- As cell phones, PDAs, and iPods are produced with more computing power, they are essentially becoming miniaturized laptops. They can be modified in the same way as any other computer.

- Security researchers converted a Sega® Dreamcast into a specialized espionage device by loading a different operating system and network tools. When connected to a company's internal network, the system was designed to create a secure connection with an attacker outside the network, allowing the attacker access to sensitive data (www.blackhat.com/html/bh-usa-02/bh-usa-02-speakers.html#Davis%20Higbee).

- DVD players have been modified to disable region restrictions to add storage capability and create networking capability.

- Access cards that have been reprogrammed or "pirated" allow people to illegally intercept and decrypt satellite television signals and receive television programming without making any payments to subscription satellite television providers. The copyrighted software on the card is modified to bypass satellite television's conditional access system and open all programming channels.

- Uninterruptible power supplies (UPS) have been modified to function as packet sniffers by installing computer components inside the cover (www.defcon.org/html/links/defcon-media-archives.html#dc-11-Attack!).

Alternate Use of Gaming Console

Modified Sega® Dreamcast that allows remote network access

Modified menu on a hacked DVD player

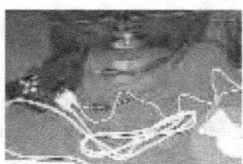

Xbox® and controller modified for use as a computer with mouse and keyboard attached

Xbox® controller showing a memory port modified to accept USB devices (e.g., keyboard, mouse)

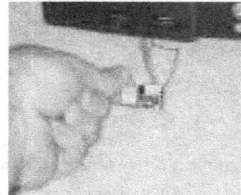

A closeup of a BIOS selector switch. The orange/brown wires coming from the LED on the right are to control a set of blue LEDs to determine what mode the unit is in. The four DIP switches are used to select which section(s) of the flashable BIOS memory is selected. The single switch next to it toggles between this Chipped BIOS and the native Xbox BIOS.

An Xbox® cracked open. The left side houses the DVD ROM drive. To the right is the 140–GB additional drive. Both devices are IDE—the Xbox® has one, and only one, primary IDE bus. Replacing the drive merely requires FAT32 partitioning, followed by copying all of the existing files over.

A TiVo® without its skin. This unit came with a single 15-GB drive. The drive was removed and replaced with two 80-GB drives, which allow the user to record about 55 hours of television. On the lower left, a network card was added, which is a 10-MB NE2k compatible ISA card, connected to the board with an intelligent st andoff card.

Appendix D. Disclosure Rules of ECPA

	Voluntary disclosure allowed?		Mechanisms to compel disclosure	
	Public Provider	Non-Public Provider	Public Provider	Non-Public Provider
Basic subscriber, session, and billing information*	Not to government, unless § 2702(c) exception applies [§ 2702(a)(3)]	Yes [§ 2702(a)(3)]	Subpoena; 2703(d) order; or warrant [§ 2703(c)(2)]	Subpoena; 2703(d) order; or warrant [§ 2703(c)(2)]
Other transactional and account records	Not to government, unless § 2702(c) exception applies [§ 2702(a)(3)]	Yes [§ 2702(a)(3)]	2703(d) order or warrant [§ 2703(c)(1)]	2703(d) order or warrant [§ 2703(c)(1)]
Retrieved communications (opened e-mail and voice mail) left with provider and other stored files**	No, unless § 2702(b) exception applies [§ 2702(a)(2)]	Yes [§ 2702(a)(2)]	Subpoena with notice; 2703(d) order with notice; or warrant [§ 2703(b)]	Subpoena; ECPA doesn't apply [§ 2711(2)]
Unretrieved communication, including e-mail and voice mail (in electronic storage more than 180 days)**	No, unless § 2702(b) exception applies [§ 2702(a)(1)]	Yes [§ 2702(a)(1)]	Subpoena with notice; 2703(d) order with notice; or warrant [§ 2703(a,b)]	Subpoena with notice; 2703(d) order with notice; or warrant [§ 2703(a,b)]
Unretrieved communication, including e-mail and voice mail (in electronic storage 180 days or less)	No, unless § 2702(b) exception applies [§ 2702(a)(1)]	Yes [§ 2702(a)(1)]	Warrant [§ 2703(a)]	Warrant [§ 2703(a)]

*See 18 U.S.C. 2703(c)(2) for listing of information covered. For telephone communications, the section includes, among other records, local and long distance connection records. For Internet connections, the section includes, among others, records of session times and durations and IP addresses assigned to the user during the session.

**Some jurisdictions and ISPs interpret the case *Theofel* v. *Farey-Jones*, 341 F.3d 978 (9th Cir. 2003), amended by 2004 WL 292101 (2004), to limit compelled disclosure under this section only to warrants

Appendix E. Sample Forms

The following forms are samples of Federal and State orders for the preservation and production of records from electronic communications service providers. These forms are intended to serve as examples only. Consult legal counsel for specific forms and instruction pertaining to your jurisdiction.

Sample Application for a Federal Order

IN THE UNITED STATES DISTRICT COURT

FOR THE WESTERN DISTRICT OF WISCONSIN

IN THE MATTER OF AN APPLICATION FOR AN ORDER PURSUANT TO TITLE 18, UNITED STATES CODE, SECTION 2703	) <u>SEALED</u>)) Case No.)))))

APPLICATION FOR PRODUCTION OF RECORDS

The United States of America, by J.B. Van Hollen, United States Attorney for the Western District of Wisconsin, by (AUSA), Assistant United States Attorney for that district, hereby applies for an order pursuant to Title 18, United States Code, Sections 2703(b)(1)(B)(ii) and (d), directing (name of company), to produce: **(SELECT INFORMATION NEEDED FROM LIST BELOW)**

A.   All customer or subscriber account information for any accounts registered to (target customer), or associated with (target customer). For each such account, the information shall include:

   1.   The subscriber's account or login name; and e-mail address;

   2.   The subscriber's address;

   3.   The subscriber's telephone number or numbers; [and local and long distance telephone connection records, or records of session times and durations;]

4. Length of service (including start date) and types of service utilized;

5. Telephone or instrument number or other subscriber number or identity, including any temporarily assigned network address; and

6. The means and source of payment for such service (including any credit card or bank account number).

B. User connection logs for:

1. All accounts identified in Part A, above;

2. The IP address (IP Address if known); and

3. For the time period beginning (date) through and including the date of this order, for any connections to or from (ISP). User connection logs should contain the following:

    1. Connection time and date;

    2. Disconnect time and date;

    3. Method of connection to system (e.g., SLIP, PPP, Shell);

    4. Data transfer volume (e.g., bytes);

    5. Connection information for other systems to which user connected via, including:

        a. Connection destination;

        b. Connection time and date;

        c. Disconnect time and date;

        d. Method of connection to system (e.g., telnet, ftp, http);

        e. Data transfer volume (e.g., bytes).

C. The contents of electronic communications (not in electronic storage [1]) that were placed or stored in (ISP) computer systems in directories or files owned or controlled by the accounts identified in Part A at any time after (Date) up through and including the date of this Order.

D. The contents of electronic communications in electronic storage for more than 180 days from the date of the Court's order.

As set forth in the following paragraphs, the United States submits that there are specific, articulable facts showing that these records and information are relevant and material to an ongoing criminal investigation.

1. (Facts of criminal investigation)

    The requested information is relevant and material to the investigation concerning (crime) because the requested information will show (insert facts).

2. The United States requests that notification to the subscriber be delayed for a period of 90 days because notification could cause an "adverse result" in this criminal investigation as that term is defined in Title 18, United States Code, Section 2705(a)(2). The United States submits that an adverse result could occur because (insert facts).

3.   WHEREFORE, the United States requests that this Court order, pursuant to Title 18, United States Code, Sections 2703(b)(1)(B)(ii) and (d), that the custodian of records for (Name of company) produce to agents of the (Agency) within ten days from the entry of this order the records described above in sections A through (letter).

The United States also requests that this Court order that the agents and employees of (Name of company) not disclose the existence of this application and order for production, or any production of records made thereunder, for a period of 90 days unless authorized by this Court. It is further requested that the Clerk of this Court seal this application and the order issued until further order of the Court.

Dated this ___ day of (Date).

Respectfully submitted,

J.B. VAN HOLLEN
United States Attorney

By:

_____

(AUSA)
Assistant U.S. Attorney

---

[1] "Electronic Storage" is defined in 18 U.S.C. § 2510(17) as "(A) any temporary, intermediate storage of a wire or electronic communication incidental to the electronic transmission thereof; and (B) any storage of such communication by an electronic communication service for purposes of backup protection of such communication." The government does not seek access to such material unless it has been in electronic storage longer than 180 days.

Sample Federal Order

IN THE UNITED STATES DISTRICT COURT

FOR THE WESTERN DISTRICT OF WISCONSIN

IN THE MATTER OF AN APPLICATION FOR AN ORDER PURSUANT TO TITLE 18, UNITED STATES CODE, SECTION 2703	) <u>SEALED</u>)) Case No.)))))

ORDER

This matter comes before the Court on the application of J.B. Van Hollen, United States Attorney for the Western District of Wisconsin, by (AUSA), Assistant United States Attorney for that district, for an order for production of records directed to (Name of company), pursuant to Title 18, United States Code, Sections 2703(b)(1)(B)(ii) and (d); specifically:

A. All customer or subscriber account information for any accounts registered to (target customer), or associated with (target customer). For each such account, the information shall include: **(SELECT INFORMATION NEEDED FROM LIST BELOW)**

    1. The subscriber's account or login name; and e-mail address;

    2. The subscriber's address;

    3. The subscriber's telephone number or numbers; [and local and long distance telephone connection records, or records of session times and durations;]

    4. Length of service (including start date) and types of service utilized;

    5. Telephone or instrument number or other subscriber number or identity, including any temporarily assigned network address; and

    6. The means and source of payment for such service (including any credit card or bank account number).

B. User connection logs for:

    1. All accounts identified in Part A, above;

    2. The IP address (IP Address if known); and

    3. For the time period beginning (Date) through and including the date of this order, for any connections to or from (ISP).

    User connection logs should contain the following:

    1. Connection time and date;

2. Disconnect time and date;

3. Method of connection to system (e.g., SLIP, PPP, Shell);

4. Data transfer volume (e.g., bytes);

5. Connection information for other systems to which user connected via, including:

    a. Connection destination;

    b. Connection time and date;

    c. Disconnect time and date;

    d. Method of connection to system (e.g., telnet, ftp, http);

    e. Data transfer volume (e.g., bytes).

C. The contents of electronic communications (not in electronic storage [2]) that were placed or stored in (ISP) computer systems in directories or files owned or controlled by the accounts identified in Part A at any time after (Date) up through and including the date of this Order.

D. The contents of electronic communications in electronic storage for more than 180 days from the date of the Court's order.

It appearing that the application is made in good faith and that there are specific, articulated facts showing that there is a reasonable belief that the requested records are relevant and material to an ongoing investigation,

IT IS HEREBY ORDERED, pursuant to Title 18, United States Code, Section 2703(d), that (Name of company) produce and deliver to agents of the (Agency), within ten days of the entry of this order, the information and records listed above.

IT IS FURTHER ORDERED pursuant to Title 18, United States Code, Section 2705, that (Name of company) and its agents and employees make no disclosure of the existence of this Application and Order for production or of any production of records made thereunder for a period of 90 days, unless authorized by this Court.

IT IS FURTHER ORDERED that the Clerk of this Court seal the application for production of records and this order until further order of this Court.

Dated this ____ day of (Date).

                            ————————————————
                            STEPHEN L. CROCKER
                            United States Magistrate Judge

---

[2] "Electronic Storage" is defined in 18 U.S.C. § 2510(17) as "(A) any temporary, intermediate storage of a wire or electronic communication incidental to the electronic transmission thereof; and any storage of such communication by an electronic communication service for purposes of backup protection of such communication." This order does not compel production of such material unless it has been in electronic storage longer than 180 days.

Sample State Search Warrant

SW# _____

STATE OF CALIFORNIA - COUNTY OF SANTA CLARA

SEARCH WARRANT AND AFFIDAVIT
(AFFIDAVIT)

Special Agent John Doe, swears under oath and declares under penalty of perjury that the facts expressed by him in this Search Warrant, Affidavit, and the attached and incorporated statement of probable cause are true and that based thereon he has probable cause to believe and does believe that the property described below is lawfully seizable pursuant to Penal Code Section 1524, as indicated below, and is now located at the location(s) set forth below. Wherefore, affiant requests that this Search Warrant be issued.

NIGHT SEARCH REQUESTED: ☐YES   ☒NO   Justification on page(s): _____

AFFIANT'S SIGNATURE: _____   **REVIEWED BY:** _____
AFTER BEING SWORN   DEPUTY DISTRICT ATTORNEY

(SEARCH WARRANT)

THE PEOPLE OF THE STATE OF CALIFORNIA TO ANY SHERIFF, POLICEMAN OR PEACE OFFICER IN THE COUNTY OF SANTA CLARA: proof by affidavit having been made before me by Special Agent John Doe, that there is probable cause to believe that the property described herein may be found at the locations set forth herein and that it is lawfully seizable pursuant to Penal Code Section 1524, as indicated below by "x"(s) in that it:

☐ was stolen or embezzled.

☒ was used as the means of committing a felony.

☐ is possessed by a person with the intent to use it as means of committing a public offense or is possessed by another to whom he or she may have delivered it for the purpose of concealing it or preventing its discovery.

☒ tends to show that a felony has been committed or that a particular person has committed a felony.

☐ tends to show that sexual exploitation of a child, in violation of Penal Code Section 311.3, has occurred or is occurring.

YOU ARE THEREFORE COMMANDED TO SEARCH THE PREMISES OF:

LOCATION:

YAHOO!   Attn: Custodian of Records
701 First Avenue
Sunnyvale, CA 94089

FOR THE FOLLOWING PROPERTY:

A.) All stored electronic communications, including e-mail, digit al images, buddy lists, and any other files associated with user accounts identified as:

roe1234@yahoo.com

B.) All connection logs and records of user activit y for each such account including:

1. Connection dates and times.

2. Disconnect dates and times.

3. Method of connection (e.g., telnet, ftp, http).

4. Data transfer volume.

5. User name associated with the connections.

6. Telephone caller identification records.

7. Any other connection information, such as the Internet Protocol address of the source of the connection.

8. Connection information for the other computer to which the user of the above-referenced accounts connected, by any means, during the connection period, including the destination IP address, connection time and date, dis - connect time and date, method of connection to the destination computer , and all other information related to the connection from Yahoo.

C.) Any other records or accounts related to the abo ve-referenced names and user names, including but not limited to, cor respondence, billing records, records of contact by any person or entity regarding the above-referenced names and user names, and any other subscr ber information, referenced name, and any other subscriber information.

NON-DISCLOSURE ORDER

It is further ordered that Yahoo! is not to notify any person (including the subscriber or customer to which the materials relate) of the existence of this order for 90 days in that such a disclosure could give the subscriber an opportunity to destroy evidence, notify confederates, or flee or continue his flight from prosecution.

[_____] The court orders the entire/designated portion of the af fidavit sealed. Said sealed
initials initials portion shall not be opened e xcept upon order of the court. Designated portion: _____

The court orders that any items seized during the lawful service of this search warrant be disposed in accordance with the law, by the Sacramento County Sheriff's Department, upon adjudication of the case. The officers serving the search warrant are also hereby authorized, without necessity of further court order, to return seized items to any known victim(s) if such items have been photographically documented.

If necessary, searching officers are authorized to employ the use of outside experts, acting under the direct control of the investigating officers, to access and preserve any computer data.

Searching officers are authorized to videotape and/or photograph the entry and search of the premises described herein, at the discretion of the searching officers.

AND TO SEIZE IT IF FOUND and bring it forthwith before me, or this court, at the court-house of this court. This Search Warrant and incorporated Affidavit was sworn to as true and subscribed before me this _____ day of _____, 2002, at _____ A.M./P.M. Wherefore, I find probable cause for the issuance of this Search Warrant and do issue it.

_____ Night search approved: YES [_____] NO [_____]
(Signature of Magistrate)   (Magistrate's Initials)

Judge of the Superior Court, Santa Clara, State of California

Executed by: _____ Date: _____ Time: _____

Affidavit in Support of Search Warrant
County of Santa Clara

Your affiant, Special Agent John Doe, is employed as a full-time, sworn law enforcement officer for the California Department of Justice and has been for the past 10 years. During your affiant's tenure, your affiant has investigated numerous cases involving financial crimes, thefts, computer- and communications-related crimes, robbery, organized crime, homicide, and narcotics. Your affiant has developed and taught required Peace Officer Standards and Training (POST) courses for technological investigations. Your affiant has also qualified as an expert witness, on multiple occasions, in several areas of electronic technology and communication. Additionally, your affiant has received advanced training in electronic crimes from the Federal Bureau of Investigation, Quantico, VA, the National Technical Investigators Association, Washington, D.C., the High Technology Crime Investigation Association, and other industry seminars.

Your affiant is currently assigned to the Sacramento Valley Hi-Tech Crimes Task Force, which operates under the auspice of the Sacramento County Sheriff's Department, and is tasked with the investigation of crimes as they relate to the illegal use, abuse, or theft of electronic service, technology, and equipment.

On September 11, 2002, your affiant received information from California Department of XYZ, Information Technology employee R. Smith, that computer servers belonging to the Department had been illegally accessed through the Internet. Smith further reported that an unauthorized program had been installed on the computers to relay information garnered from the system to the E-mail account, roe1234@yahoo.com. Smith provided the following statement:

> Two California Department of XYZ (DOX) computer systems are responsible for the function of DNS (Domain Name Services) and the system responsible for relaying mail to and from the Internet and GroupWise have been compromised by a hacker. The attack on these systems started at approximately 1825 hours on September 7, 2002.

> The attack was detected by a file system baseline utility program (Tripwire), installed on the Unix systems outside the firewall. This attack has resulted in a disruption in statewide Internet e-mail for this department. The hacker was able to capture system information as well as keystrokes, including usernames and passwords, and mailed this information to his private Internet account on Yahoo. Had this event not been detected, the hacker would have been able to capture and monitor DOB Internet traffic.

> The method of attack looks to be that of a knowledgeable adversary. There were very few traces of the activity left on the systems. The Tripwire software reported that several file links were removed and that some binary files (Programs) were modified. There were also scripts placed on the systems to log the keystrokes and e-mail them back to the responsible party (hacker). At this time we believe the e-mail address of the hacker to be roe1234@yahoo.com.

> The connection logs of the system point to activity from several different sources including France, Yugoslavia, Italy, and New York. The time of the incident and the connection log points to New York (64.95.2.154) as the possible source.

Your affiant knows that individuals involved in illegal accessing of computers (hacking) will frequently illegally access computer systems through the Internet and install programs to either illegally control systems, destroy data, or obtain data. Your affiant also knows that such an act is a felony under California state law (Pen. Code sec. 502 (c)(1)) and that the nexus of the crime can be at any point of origination or termination within the state of California. Your affiant is aware that yahoo.com is located within the County of Santa Clara, State of California.

Through experience and training, your affiant knows companies offering e-mail services, such as yahoo.com, maintain records related to account registration, connection time and dates, Internet routing information (Internet Protocol numbers), and message content, that may assist in the identification of person/s accessing and utilizing the account.

Based on the aforementioned information, your affiant believes sufficient probable cause exists for the issuance of a search warrant for:

The following location:

A business, operated under the name of yahoo.com, located at 701 First Ave., Sunnyvale, CA.

For the following items:

All stored electronic communications, including e-mail, digital images, buddy lists, and any other files associated with user accounts identified as:

roe1234@yahoo.com

All connection logs and records of user activity for each such account, including:

1. Connection dates and times.
2. Disconnect dates and times.
3. Method of connection (e.g., telnet, ftp, http).
4. Data transfer volume.
5. User name associated with the connections.
6. Telephone caller identification records.
7. Any other connection information, such as the Internet Protocol address of the source of the connection.
8. Connection information for the other computer to which the user of the above-referenced accounts connected, by any means, during the connection period, including the destination IP address, connection time and date, disconnect time and date, method of connection to the destination computer, and all other information related to the connection from Yahoo.

Any other records or accounts related to the above-referenced names and user names, including but not limited to, correspondence, billing records, records of contact by any person or entity regarding the above-referenced names and user names, and any other subscriber information, referenced name, and any other subscriber information.

Affiant further requests that Yahoo! be ordered not to notify any person (including the subscriber or customer to which the materials relate) of the existence of this order for 90 days. Affiant submits that such an order is justified because notification of the existence of this order could seriously jeopardize the ongoing investigation. Such a disclosure could give the subscr ber an opportunity to destroy evidence, notify confederates, or flee or continue his flight from prosecution.

Your affiant swears the aforementioned information is truthful and accurate, to the best of his knowledge.

_____
Special Agent John Doe, Affiant

Sample Language for Preservation Request Letters Under 18 U.S.C. § 2703(f)

[Internet Service Provider]
[Address]
VIA FAX to (xxx) xxx-xxxx

Dear:

I am writing to [confirm our telephone conversation earlier today and to] make a formal request for the preservation of records and other evidence pursuant to 18 U.S.C. § 2703(f) pending further legal process.

You are hereby requested to preserve, for a period of 90 days, the records described below currently in your possession, including records stored on backup media, in a form that includes the complete record. You also are requested not to disclose the existence of this request to the subscriber or any other person, other than as necessary to comply with this request. If compliance with this request may result in a permanent or temporary termination of service to the accounts described below, or otherwise alert the subscriber or user of these accounts as to your actions to preserve the referenced files and records, please contact me before taking such actions.

This request applies only retrospectively. It does not in any way obligate you to capture and preserve new information that arises after the date of this request.

This preservation request applies to the following records and evidence:

A. All stored communications and other files reflecting communications to or from [E-mail Account/User Name/IP Address or Domain Name (between DATE1 at TIME1 and DATE2 at TIME2)];

B. All files that have been accessed by [E-mail Account/User Name/IP Address or Domain Name (between DATE1 at TIME1 and DATE2 at TIME2)] or are controlled by user accounts associated with [E-mail Account/User Name/IP Address or Domain Name (between DATE1 at TIME1 and DATE2 at TIME2)];

C. All connection logs and records of user activity for [E-mail Account/User Name/IP Address or Domain Name (between DATE1 at TIME1 and DATE2 at TIME2)], including;

1. Connection date and time.

2. Disconnect date and time.

3. Method of connection (e.g., telnet, ftp, http).

4. Type of connection (e.g., modem, cable/DSL, T1/LAN).

5. Data transfer volume.

6. User name associated with the connection and other connection information, including the Internet Protocol address of the source of the connection.

7. Telephone caller identification records;

8. Records of files or system attributes accessed, modified, or added by the user;

9. Connection information for other computers to which the user of the [E-mail Account/User Name/IP Address or Domain Name (between DATE1 at TIME1 and DATE2 at TIME2)] connected, by any means, during the connection period, including the destination IP address, connection time and date, disconnect time and date, method of connection to the destination computer, the identities (account and screen names) and subscriber information, if known, for any person or entity to which such connection information relates, and all other information related to the connection from ISP or its subsidiaries.

All records and other evidence relating to the subscriber(s), customer(s), account holder(s), or other entity(ies) associated with [E-mail Account/User Name/IP Address or Domain Name (between DATE1 at TIME1 and DATE2 at TIME2)], including, without limitation, subscriber names, user names, screen names or other identities, mailing addresses, residential addresses, business addresses, e-mail addresses and other contact information, telephone numbers or other subscriber number or identifier number, billing records, information about the length of service and the types of services the subscriber or customer utilized, and any other identifying information, whether such records or other evidence are in electronic or other form.

Any other records and other evidence relating to [E-mail Account/User Name/IP Address or Domain Name (between DATE1 at TIME1 and DATE2 at TIME2)]. Such records and other evidence include, without limitation, correspondence and other records of contact by any person or entity about the above-referenced account, the content and connection logs associated with or relating to postings, communications and any other activities to or through [E-mail Account/User Name/IP Address or Domain Name (between DATE1 at TIME1 and DATE2 at TIME2)], whether such records or other evidence are in electronic or other form.

Very truly yours,

_____

Appendix F. References

American Society of Crime Laboratory Directors (ASCLD)
http://ascld.org

American Society for Information Science & Technology (ASIS&T)
www.asis.org

Communications Fraud and Control Association (CFCA)
www.cfca.org

Computer Crime and Intellectual Property Section (CCIPS), U.S. Department of Justice
www.cybercrime.gov

Computer Forensic Investigators Digest (CFID)
www.forensicsweb.com

Defense Computer Forensics Laboratory (DCFL)
www.dc3mil/dcci/dcci.htm

Defense Cyber Crime Institute (DCCI)
www.dc3mil/dcfl/dcfl.htm

European Working Party on Information Technology Crime (Interpol)
www.interpol.int/Public/TechnologyCrime/
    WorkingParties/Default.asp#europa

Financial Crimes Enforcement Network (FinCEN)
http://www.fincen.gov

High Tech Crime Consortium (HTCC)
http://www.hightechcrimecops.org

High-Technology Crime Investigation Association (HTCIA)
http://htcia.org
For local chapter information, see the Web site.

Lathe Gambit (NATO Forensic Organization)
www.650mi.nato.army.mil

Magloclen
www.iir.com/riss/magloclen

National Security Institute (NSI)
http://nsi.org

National Technical Investigators Association (NATIA)
www.natia.org

National White Collar Crime Center (NW3C)
www.nw3c.org

SEARCH
http://search.org

Appendix G. List of Reviewing Organizations

The following is a list of organizations to which a draft copy of this document was mailed.

Alaska Criminal Laboratory

America Online–Investigations and Law Enforcement Affairs

American Prosecutors Research Institute

American Society of Law Enforcement Trainers

Bureau of Alcohol, Tobacco, Firearms and Explosives–Computer Forensics Branch

Center for Law and Computers, Chicago-Kent College of Law, Illinois Institute of Technology

Chicago Regional Computer Forensics Laboratory

Computer Forensics Inc.

Computer Science and Telecommunications Board

Criminal Justice Institute

Drug Enforcement Administration–Digital Evidence Laboratory

Federal Bar Association

Federal Bureau of Investigation

Federal Law Enforcement Training Center–Financial Fraud Institute

Georgia Bureau of Investigation, Intelligence Unit

Hawaii County Police

Heart of America Regional Computer Forensics Laboratory

Intermountain West Regional Computer Forensics Laboratory

Miami Valley Regional Computer Forensics Laboratory

The MITRE Corporation

National Center for Forensic Science

National Computer Security Association (TruSecure)

National Law Enforcement and Corrections Technology Center–West

North Texas Regional Computer Forensics Laboratory

Northwest Regional Computer Forensics Laboratory

Ohio Bureau of Criminal ID and Investigation

Regional Computer Forensic Laboratory National Program Office

Rocky Mountain Regional Computer Forensics Laboratory

San Diego Regional Computer Forensic Laboratory

SEARCH Group, Inc.

Silicon Valley Regional Computer Forensic
Laboratory

Social Security Administration–Office of
the Inspector General, Office of
Investigations

U.S. Department of Defense Cyber Crime
Center

U.S. Department of Justice–Computer
Crime and Intellectual Property Section

U.S. Department of Justice–Western
District of Michigan

U.S. Naval Criminal Investigative Service

U.S. Postal Service, Office of Inspector
General

Wyoming Division of Criminal
Investigations

Index

About the National Institute of Justice

NIJ is the research, development, and evaluation agency of the U.S. Department of Justice. The Institute's mission is to advance scientific research, development, and evaluation to enhance the administration of justice and public safety. NIJ's principal authorities are derived from the Omnibus Crime Control and Safe Streets Act of 1968, as amended (see 42 U.S.C. §§ 3721–3723).

The NIJ Director is appointed by the President and confirmed by the Senate. The Director establishes the Institute's objectives, guided by the priorities of the Office of Justice Programs, the U.S. Department of Justice, and the needs of the field. The Institute actively solicits the views of criminal justice and other professionals and researchers to inform its search for the knowledge and tools to guide policy and practice.

Strategic Goals

NIJ has seven strategic goals grouped into three categories:

Creating relevant knowledge and tools

1. Partner with State and local practitioners and policymakers to identify social science research and technology needs.
2. Create scientific, relevant, and reliable knowledge—with a particular emphasis on terrorism, violent crime, drugs and crime, cost-effectiveness, and community-based efforts—to enhance the administration of justice and public safety.
3. Develop affordable and effective tools and technologies to enhance the administration of justice and public safety.

Dissemination

4. Disseminate relevant knowledge and information to practitioners and policymakers in an understandable, timely, and concise manner.
5. Act as an honest broker to identify the information, tools, and technologies that respond to the needs of stakeholders.

Agency management

6. Practice fairness and openness in the research and development process.
7. Ensure professionalism, excellence, accountability, cost-effectiveness, and integrity in the management and conduct of NIJ activities and programs.

Program Areas

In addressing these strategic challenges, the Institute is involved in the following program areas: crime control and prevention, including policing; drugs and crime; justice systems and offender behavior, including corrections; violence and victimization; communications and information technologies; critical incident response; investigative and forensic sciences, including DNA; less-than-lethal technologies; officer protection; education and training technologies; testing and standards; technology assistance to law enforcement and corrections agencies; field testing of promising programs; and international crime control.

In addition to sponsoring research and development and technology assistance, NIJ evaluates programs, policies, and technologies. NIJ communicates its research and evaluation findings through conferences and print and electronic media.

To find out more about the National Institute of Justice, please visit:

www.ojp.usdoj.gov/nij

or contact:

National Criminal Justice
 Reference Service
P.O. Box 6000
Rockville, MD 20849–6000
800–851–3420
e-mail: *askncjrs@ncjrs.org*

www.ingramcontent.com/pod-product-compliance
Lightning Source LLC
Chambersburg PA
CBHW081448170526
45166CB00008B/2351